Gennaro's
FAST COOK ITALIAN

First published in the United Kingdom in 2018 by
Pavilion
43 Great Ormond Street
London WC1N 3HZ

ISBN: 978-1-91159-511-3

A CIP catalogue record for this book is available from the
British Library.

10 9 8 7 6 5 4 3 2 1

Reproduction by Mission, Hong Kong
Printed and bound by Toppan Leefung Printing Ltd, China

This book can be ordered direct from the publisher at
www.pavilionbooks.com

Gennaro's
FAST COOK ITALIAN

FROM FRIDGE TO FORK IN 40 MINUTES OR LESS

Gennaro Contaldo

PAVILION

CONTENTS

ITALIAN FAST COOKING

Fast cooking doesn't have to mean unhealthy fast food! In fact, quite the opposite! The Italian philosophy of using a few good ingredients and cooking them in a simple, unfussy way means you can create beautiful, nutritious dishes in no time. Traditionally, some of the best Italian dishes are made quickly with just a few fresh or stored ingredients.

These days, not all Italians have the time to cook lengthy meals like they used to – gone are the days when women stayed at home and made pasta by hand, or soaked pulses in preparation for a slow-cooked pot of soup or stew. Don't get me wrong, I, like most Italians, still love to cook like this, but perhaps at weekends or for festivities like Christmas and Easter, when I have more time to cook. During a normal week, when the family is at work and school, there just isn't the time to prepare the dishes that our grandmothers once made.

Italians mainly cook from scratch and use high-quality, seasonal ingredients. This doesn't mean starting to cook the night before, but a little planning in advance to ensure you have the right ingredients in your store cupboard is a good start. Take pasta or risotto, for example; these two classic staples of Italian cooking, so quick and simple to prepare, make excellent, nutritious meals that everyone can enjoy at any time. I always make sure I have a selection of dried pasta in the cupboard, as well as risotto rice, good olive oil, stock (bouillon) and cans of tomatoes. Add some onions, carrots, garlic, pancetta and Parmesan from the fridge and I can already see quite a few meals. Even when the cupboard is bare, a quick dish of *Spaghetti aglio, olio e peperoncino* (garlic, oil and chilli) is a popular standby especially among Italian youngsters who opt for it as a midnight snack after a night on the town!

Of course, Italian food is not just pasta and there are so many meat, fish and vegetable dishes that can be prepared in little time. Fish, chicken, thin slices of meat as well as eggs for delicious omelettes cook in no time and provide nourishing meals. Vegetables are also often used in the Italian kitchen to create delicious main dishes which cook quickly. Italian cooking doesn't need too many added flavours, sauces or marinades, as Italians prefer to buy fresh, quality ingredients which speak for themselves! Take a simple steak, for example – as long as you buy the best piece of meat you can afford, just a little salt and pepper and some oil are all that you really need; while the steak

is grilling (broiling) or frying, slice some tomatoes and red onions for a side salad. Serve with some good bread and you have a delicious meal fit for a king, which has taken far less time to prepare than waiting for a takeaway to arrive! And, of course, it is far more nutritious and enjoyable to eat!

To make life even simpler, there are all sorts of short cuts available these days; walk into any supermarket and you will find a wide variety of ready-chopped and spiralised vegetables as well as cubed pancetta, grated cheeses, canned beans and pulses. Italian delis stock good-quality fresh sauces like pesto, tomato sauce and many others, as well as mouth-watering pickled vegetables in jars, which are always handy to keep in your store cupboard. You can of course make your own sauces; it's always a good idea to make a large quantity of say tomato sauce perhaps once a month (time-permitting) and freeze in batches to use whenever required. On a weekly basis, if you have time, you could chop or grate a few basic vegetables, like onions, carrots, celery, courgettes (zucchini), garlic and so on, store them in containers in the fridge and use them in your cooking throughout the week. You could also grate a quantity of Parmesan cheese and chop pieces of pancetta so you have these to hand, too. This way, you know you will be using the freshest ingredients for all your dishes as well as reducing so much of your preparation time when it comes to cooking. In fact, a little planning ahead at the beginning of the week will make cooking easier, stress free and will ensure healthy balanced meals at all times with minimum fuss and effort.

Overleaf, you will find my list of essentials for your store cupboard and fridge, which will give you more than enough for quick and simple meals at any time. Obviously, add some meat and fish to this and your meal planning will be sorted.

All the recipes in this book have been carefully chosen to ensure they are quick and effortless to prepare and cook. They are all super simple to follow and even someone with only basic cooking skills will be able to make them. Although perfect for everyday cooking, most of the recipes can also be made for special occasions – why spend hours in the kitchen just because you have guests coming or you are making a celebratory meal?

I hope you enjoy cooking the recipes in this book, which I hope will prove invaluable not just for when you are looking for a quick dish to rustle up, but for all your daily meals – simple recipes for life that can be used over and over again.

Enjoy, happy cooking and *buon appetito*!

GENNARO

MY ITALIAN KITCHEN ESSENTIALS

I have put together a basic list of essential Italian ingredients, which I believe will help you in your meal planning. Keep an eye on your supplies and when something runs out, make sure it is replaced.

STORE CUPBOARD

Extra virgin olive oil, for dressing
Olive oil or vegetable oil, for frying
Anchovies
Capers
Dried porcini
Green and black olives
Dried oregano
Dried chilli (hot red pepper) flakes
Natural breadcrumbs
Chopped walnuts
Sea salt and black pepper
Jars of good-quality preserved vegetables – aubergines (eggplants), courgettes (zucchini), (bell) peppers, artichokes, sun-dried tomatoes
Dried pasta – a selection of long and short varieties
Vegetable stock (bouillon) – I also like to keep chicken, beef and fish stock, but as long as you have a supply of vegetable stock, you can make most dishes
Red or white wine vinegar
Wine – red and white
Pesto
Plain (all-purpose) flour
Risotto rice and long-grain rice
Quick-cook polenta (fine cornmeal)
Cans of beans and pulses – cannellini, borlotti (cranberry) beans, chickpeas (garbanzo beans), lentils
Cans of chopped tomatoes and passata (strained tomatoes)
Grissini breadsticks
Pane carasau (wafer-thin Sardinian flatbread)

FRIDGE

Parmesan
Ricotta
Mascarpone
Mozzarella – bufala to enjoy fresh in salads or starters and a harder variety for cooking with
Pancetta or bacon
Prosciutto – this usually has a good sell-by date and is handy to keep for a quick antipasto or snack
Organic free-range eggs
Good-quality gnocchi from a deli

FREEZER

Peas
Broad (fava) beans
Berries
Homemade tomato sauce (see p.185)

FRESH PRODUCE

Onions – white and red
Garlic
Red chilli
Carrots
Celery
Courgettes (zucchini)
Potatoes
Salad – gem lettuce and salad leaves
Tomatoes
Selection of (bell) peppers
Herbs – parsley, rosemary, sage, thyme, mint

SALADS

Salads have come a long way from the days of unappetizing, limp lettuce leaves and tasteless tomatoes. Salad dressings have evolved too, and now interesting ingredients are put together to make delicious salads that don't necessarily have to be eaten as a side dish, but can also be enjoyed as a main course.

Italians love salads and most meals include a salad of some sort – it could be chargrilled (bell) peppers with garlic and olive oil, or thinly sliced courgettes (zucchini) with white wine vinegar and fresh mint, or simply a mix of seasonal green leaves. *Prosciutto crudo* is probably one of Italy's most loved and well-known ingredients. Although here in the UK it is known simply as 'prosciutto', in Italy prosciutto means 'ham', which can be either *cotto* (cooked) or *crudo* (raw or cured). It marries very well with fruit – melon is probably the one that always springs to mind; I must admit this is one of my favourite combinations, especially during the summer when cantaloupe melon is at its most refreshing (see the recipe on p.32). Figs are also a firm favourite and so are peaches, again, during the summer months, when they are at their best. Autumnal fruits such as plums, apples and pears all make delicious combinations.

Dressings in Italy tend to be delicate and uncomplicated, and the classic olive oil and vinegar, or olive oil and lemon juice, are still my favourites. Always use good-quality extra-virgin olive oil and wine vinegar, and dress your salads just before serving to avoid soggy leaves. I tend to sprinkle a little salt over my salads first, before adding two parts olive oil to one part vinegar or lemon juice.

Most of the salads in this book are also suitable to enjoy as starters, or to serve at parties or as accompaniments to a barbeque. They are a light and enjoyable way to pack in your 'five a day', so, whether you serve them as an accompaniment or as a main course, you can be sure you are eating a healthy, nutritious dish.

INSALATA DI GAMBERI E ASPARAGI

PRAWN AND ASPARAGUS SALAD

A quick and healthy salad, which can be eaten as a light lunch or served as an antipasto with some good bread.

Cooking time: 12–15 minutes

Serves 4

250 g/9 oz asparagus tips
2 tbsp extra-virgin olive oil
1 garlic clove, finely chopped
1 tbsp finely chopped parsley
300 g/10½ oz raw king prawns
   (jumbo shrimp)
juice and peeled zest of 1 lemon,
   zest finely chopped
20 g/¾ oz/1 generous tbsp butter
sea salt and freshly ground black pepper

Bring a saucepan of water to the boil, add the asparagus tips and simmer for about 3 minutes, until just tender. Drain and set aside.

Meanwhile, in a frying pan (skillet) set over a medium heat, heat the olive oil, add the garlic and parsley, and sweat for 1 minute. Add the prawns and stir-fry for a couple of minutes, until cooked. Stir in the chopped lemon zest and juice, remove from the heat and set aside.

In another frying pan, melt the butter, add the cooked asparagus, season with some salt and pepper, and stir-fry for 1 minute. Remove from the heat, then arrange on a serving dish, together with the cooked prawns, pouring over the pan juices.

INSALATA DI FAGIOLINI
GREEN BEAN SALAD

This lovely, crunchy salad can be eaten warm or cold, and so can be made in advance, if desired. It makes a lovely accompaniment to grilled meat, fish or frittata. If you prefer a less-strong dressing, then simply reduce the amount of mustard. To save time, buy ready-trimmed green beans.

Cooking time: 10 minutes

Serves 2–4

180 g/6¼ oz green (French) beans, trimmed
160 g/5¾ oz sugar snap peas
½ red onion, or 1 banana shallot

For the dressing:
1 small garlic clove
2 tbsp extra-virgin olive oil
1 tbsp red wine vinegar
1 tsp mustard
sea salt, to taste

Place the green beans in a large saucepan, cover with water, and bring to the boil. Reduce the heat and simmer for about 6 minutes, then add the sugar snaps and continue to cook for a couple of minutes, until tender. Make sure not to overcook the vegetables. Drain and set aside.

Meanwhile, finely slice the onion or shallot and set aside.

Make the dressing. Finely chop the garlic and combine with the olive oil, vinegar, mustard and a little salt, to taste.

Place the drained vegetables in a bowl, add the onion or shallot, and pour over the dressing to serve.

INSALATA DI PATATE

WARM POTATO SALAD WITH RED ONION AND MINT

In Italy, when Italians make potato salad, they usually flavour it with dried oregano. Here, to give the salad a fresh summery flavour, I have added fresh mint. Marinating the onions while waiting for the potatoes to cook gives a nice vinegary kick to the dish and, unless you really like lots of vinegar, you don't need to add any more to the salad. However, don't get rid of the vinegar marinade, because you can use it again. You could also marinate more onions than you need, keep them in the fridge, and use them to liven up other salads or sandwiches.

Cooking time: 12 minutes

Serves 4

400 g/14 oz baby potatoes, washed,
    skins kept on
1 small red onion
sea salt and freshly ground black pepper
10 tbsp white wine vinegar
3 tbsp extra-virgin olive oil
12 mint leaves, roughly chopped, to serve

Boil the potatoes in a large saucepan for about 10 minutes, until tender.

Meanwhile, finely slice the onion and place in a small bowl with a pinch of salt and cover with the vinegar.

Drain the potatoes and place in a serving bowl. Drain the marinated onions and add to the potatoes, mixing in gently. Drizzle with olive oil, season with salt and pepper and scatter over the chopped mint leaves, to serve.

INSALATA DI FAVE E CARCIOFI

BROAD BEAN AND ARTICHOKE SALAD, WITH ROCKET AND PARMESAN

A quick and simple salad using preserved artichokes, which are obtainable from good Italian delis, and convenient frozen broad beans, which are lightly cooked until tender. It can be served as a starter, as a side dish to lamb dishes (see Anchovy-Infused Lamb Cutlets, p.122) or as a light lunch with some crusty bread.

Cooking time: 10 minutes

Serves 2–4

100 g/3½ oz/⅔ cup frozen shelled broad
  (fava) beans
20 g/¾ oz/2½ tbsp pine nuts
150 g/5½ oz artichoke hearts preserved in oil,
  drained
2 handfuls of rocket (arugula)
30 g/1 oz Parmesan, shaved

For the dressing:
2 tbsp extra-virgin olive oil
juice of ½ lemon
sea salt, to taste

Bring a small saucepan of water to the boil over a medium heat, add the broad beans, bring back to the boil and cook for 3 minutes.

Meanwhile, heat a small frying pan (skillet) over a medium heat and toast the pine nuts for about 3 minutes. Remove from the heat and set aside to cool.

Drain the cooked broad beans in a colander, then rinse them under a cold running tap to cool them down and drain well. Place the beans in a bowl, together with the artichokes, rocket, cooled pine nuts and Parmesan shavings.

Combine the dressing ingredients, pour over the salad, mix well and serve.

CARPACCIO DI ZUCCHINI

COURGETTE CARPACCIO WITH PECORINO, MINT AND POMEGRANATE

Courgettes are so versatile and, when used raw, make a lovely starter or side salad. Make sure you use very fresh courgettes and slice them as thinly as you can. Ready-to-use pomegranate seeds are widely available in supermarkets all year round and not only look great, but also make a nutritious addition to this simple, delicious dish.

Preparation time: 15 minutes

Serves 4

2 courgettes (zucchini)
4 tbsp extra-virgin olive oil
2 tbsp white wine vinegar
1 garlic clove, very finely chopped
1 tbsp finely chopped fresh mint, plus a few
    extra leaves for garnish
sea salt, to taste
50 g/1¾ oz/⅓ cup pomegranate seeds
30 g/1 oz Pecorino, shaved

Using a vegetable peeler or a mandolin, slice thin slivers of courgette lengthways and set aside.

Combine the olive oil, white wine vinegar, garlic and chopped mint, with some salt to taste, and whisk for a minute or so, until the mixture thickens slightly.

Dip the courgette slices in the dressing, then arrange on a serving plate. Pour over the remaining dressing, scatter over pomegranate seeds and Pecorino shavings, then garnish with the extra mint leaves and serve.

INSALATA DI RISO VENERE

BLACK RICE SALAD

This unusual wholefood rice, with its highly beneficial health properties, is becoming increasingly popular in Italy, appearing on restaurant menus and on supermarket shelves. Originating in China, black rice was favoured by ancient emperors for its nutritional and aphrodisiacal properties, hence the name *venere* (deriving from Venus). It is now cultivated in the rice fields of northern Italy. It is a perfect rice for salads and makes a delicious, healthy lunch or, if made in a larger quantity, is ideal to serve at parties.

Cooking time: 20–25 minutes

Serves 4

300 g/10½ oz/1½ cups black rice (*riso venere*)
½ red (bell) pepper, finely chopped
½ yellow (bell) pepper, finely chopped
2 avocados, finely chopped
6 cherry tomatoes, quartered
200 g/7 oz mozzarella or feta, cut into
    small cubes
about 12 chives, finely chopped
50 g/1¾ oz/⅓ cup pomegranate seeds
6 tbsp extra-virgin olive oil
juice of 1 lemon
sea salt, to taste

Place the rice in a saucepan with double its volume of cold water (about 700 ml/24 fl oz/3 cups). Place over a medium heat, bring to the boil, then turn the heat down and gently simmer for 15–17 minutes, until *al dente*.

Meanwhile, prepare the vegetables, mozzarella and chives.

Drain the rice, rinse under a cold running tap to cool, then drain well again. Place in a serving bowl, together with the vegetables, mozzarella, chives and pomegranate seeds. Drizzle with the olive oil and lemon juice, sprinkle over some salt, to taste, and mix together well.

INSALATA DI CECI

CHICKPEA SALAD WITH OLIVES, AMALFI LEMON AND MINT

This simple, fresh salad can be served as part of an antipasto or eaten as a main course with some bread. If made in a large quantity, it is perfect to serve at parties. Choose good-quality olives and if you can't find Amalfi lemons, buy the best you can afford for maximum taste.

Preparation time: 10 minutes

Serves 2–4

1 large Amalfi lemon
1 × 400-g/14-oz can of chickpeas (garbanzo
    beans), drained
¼ rosemary sprig
¼ thyme sprig
200 g/7 oz/2 cups mixed green and black
    stoned (pitted) olives (Kalamata and Gaeta
    types, if possible)
a small handful of fresh mint leaves,
    roughly torn
¼ fresh red chilli, finely chopped
2 tbsp extra-virgin olive oil
sea salt, to taste

Slice the lemon in half. Take one half, squeeze the juice, and set aside. Thinly slice the other lemon half, and cut each slice into quarters.

In a serving bowl, place the drained chickpeas, rosemary, thyme, whole olives, lemon slices, mint, and chilli. Drizzle with the olive oil, the lemon juice and add some salt, to taste. Mix together well and serve.

INSALATA DI PISELLI FRESCHI E BURRATA

FRESH PEA AND BURRATA SALAD, WITH SUNFLOWER-SEED CROSTINI

This is a lovely salad to make during the spring, when fresh peas are available. For speed, you can buy ready-podded peas. Burrata is a fresh cheese from Puglia which looks like mozzarella but has a very creamy interior. Good Italian delis will stock it, but if you prefer, you can use *bufala* (buffalo) mozzarella instead. This dish makes a fantastic starter or can be enjoyed as a delicious, light lunch, accompanied by the crostini.

Cooking time: 15 minutes

Serves 4

175 g/6 oz fresh peas, podded weight
85 g/3 oz watercress
leaves of 2 Gem lettuce hearts
250 g/9 oz burrata, or buffalo mozzarella

For the crostini:
50 g/1¾ oz/⅓ cup sunflower seeds
a handful of fresh basil leaves
1 tbsp extra-virgin olive oil
a pinch of sea salt
a pinch of dried chilli (hot red pepper) flakes
4 slices of good-quality crusty, seeded
    wholemeal bread, toasted

For the dressing:
2 tbsp extra-virgin olive oil
1 tbsp lemon juice
sea salt and freshly ground black pepper

Bring a saucepan of water to the boil, add the peas and cook for about 2 minutes, until tender but not overcooked. Drain, rinse under cold running water and drain well.

Meanwhile, prepare the crostini. Place the sunflower seeds, basil leaves and olive oil in a blender or food processor and whiz until you obtain a smooth consistency. Combine with the salt and chilli flakes. Toast the bread and spread with the sunflower seed paste. Set aside.

Combine the dressing ingredients.

Arrange the watercress and Gem lettuce leaves on a large serving plate, sprinkle over the cooked peas, and pour over half of the dressing. Gently break up the burrata or mozzarella and scatter over the greens. Drizzle with the remaining dressing and serve with the crostini on the side.

INSALATA DI POMODORI MISTI
OREGANO-INFUSED MIXED TOMATO SALAD

A tomato salad, such as this one, was often served during the summer when I was a child growing up in southern Italy. Tomatoes were nearly always served with local, dried oregano and fresh basil. Simply dressed, with good extra-virgin olive oil and salt, I could easily eat this every day during the summer, served with some *fresella* (double-baked bread). *Cipolotti* are large spring onions (scallions) and can sometimes be found in markets here. Alternatively, substitute with some chopped spring onions.

Preparation time: 5 minutes

Serves 2–4

500 g/1 lb 2 oz good-quality mixed tomatoes
    (red, yellow, orange)
1 cipolotto onion or 2 large spring onions
    (scallions), finely sliced
1 garlic clove, very finely chopped
a pinch of dried oregano
½ handful of basil leaves
3 tbsp extra-virgin olive oil
sea salt, to taste

Slice the tomatoes and arrange on a serving dish or in a bowl. Scatter over the sliced onion, garlic, oregano and basil. Drizzle with olive oil, add salt to taste, then mix well and serve.

INSALATA DI LENTICCHIE

LENTIL SALAD

You could make this with ready-cooked canned lentils, but I prefer to use dried, which only take about 20 minutes if you get the quick-cook variety. *Giardiniera* are preserved mixed vegetables, which can be bought in jars from Italian delis; their crunchy texture and slight sharpness from the vinegar combines perfectly with the lentils. Ensure you buy good-quality firm tomatoes, otherwise you could just add more of the *giardiniera*, if you prefer. Serve with some good rustic bread for a delicious, healthy meal at any time. It can be enjoyed both warm or cold, so is also ideal as a packed lunch or to take on picnics.

Cooking time: 25 minutes

Serves 4

200 g/7 oz/1 cup quick-cook dried brown
    or green lentils
1 garlic clove, left whole and squashed
3 whole thyme sprigs, plus the leaves from
    2 sprigs
200 g/7 oz *giardiniera* (Italian mixed
    preserved vegetables)
8 baby plum tomatoes
5 tbsp extra-virgin olive oil
sea salt and freshly ground black pepper

Place the dried lentils in a heavy-based saucepan filled with cold water, together with the squashed garlic clove and 3 whole thyme sprigs. Bring to the boil and simmer for about 20 minutes over a medium heat, until cooked (check the instructions on the packet).

Meanwhile, drain the *giardiniera* vegetables and slice the tomatoes.

Drain the lentils, discarding the garlic and thyme, and leave to cool slightly. Place the cooled lentils in a serving dish, together with the *giardiniera* and tomatoes. Add the olive oil and fresh thyme leaves, season with salt and pepper and mix well.

INSALATA DI SPECK CROCCANTE, MELA VERDE E NOCI

CRISPY SPECK, GREEN APPLE AND WALNUT SALAD

The slight saltiness of speck combined with the crunchy walnuts and fresh lemony apples makes this a delightful starter or light lunch. Make sure you place the sliced apples in acidulated water first, to avoid them going brown.

Cooking time: 20 minutes

Serves 4

2 tart green apples, e.g. Granny Smith
juice of 1 lemon
1 large Gem lettuce
100 g/3½ oz Italian speck
   (smoked, air-dried ham)
4 tbsp extra-virgin olive oil
sea salt and freshly ground black pepper
50 g/1¾ oz/⅓ cup roughly chopped walnuts
35 g/1¼ oz Parmesan, shaved

Wash the apples, core them and cut into thin slices. Place the slices in a bowl of acidulated water (water combined with half of the lemon juice) and set aside.

Roughly chop the Gem lettuce and arrange on a serving platter.

Slice the speck into thin strips. Heat 1 tbsp of the olive oil in a frying pan (skillet) over a medium heat, add the speck slices and stir-fry until crispy, but be careful not to let them burn. Remove and drain on paper towels.

Combine the remaining olive oil with the remaining lemon juice in a large bowl, season with some salt and pepper, and whisk with a fork until slightly thickened. Drain the apples well, pat dry with paper towels, and add them to the dressing mixture, tossing well.

Arrange the apples over the Gem lettuce on the platter, pouring over any remaining dressing. Sprinkle over the walnuts and cooked speck, and top with Parmesan shavings.

PROSCIUTTO E MELONE

PROSCIUTTO WITH CANTALOUPE MELON

Preparation time: 10 minutes

Serves 4

1 large cantaloupe melon
a handful of rocket (arugula) leaves
1 tbsp extra-virgin olive oil
1½ tsp balsamic vinegar
sea salt, to taste
8 slices of prosciutto (Parma ham), about
   125 g/4½ oz
8 grissini (breadsticks)

Slice the melon in half and discard the seeds. Slice the melon into segments or chunks. Set aside.

Dress the rocket in the olive oil and balsamic vinegar. Add salt, to taste.

Wrap the prosciutto slices around the grissini.

Arrange the dressed rocket and melon on a large serving platter with the prosciutto-wrapped grissini.

BRUSCHETTE CON PESCHE E PROSCIUTTO

BRUSCHETTA OF PEACHES AND PROSCIUTTO

Cooking time: 12 minutes

Serves 4

100 ml/3½ fl oz/7 tbsp white wine
2 tsp granulated sugar
8 fresh mint leaves
2 peaches, cut into quarters
4 slices of country-style bread (any will do,
   but Pugliese-style or sourdough are good)
extra-virgin olive oil, for drizzling
4 slices of prosciutto (Parma ham)

Place the white wine, sugar and 4 of the mint leaves in a small saucepan and place over a low–medium heat. Simmer for about 5 minutes, until the mixture reduces by about half. Do not let the mixture boil.

Meanwhile, heat a frying pan (skillet) or griddle pan over a low–medium heat and lightly toast the peaches for about 5 minutes, turning them over so that all the sides get some colour.

Toast the slices of bread, drizzle with a little olive oil, then top with the roasted peaches and prosciutto slices. Finally, drizzle over the reduced wine sauce and garnish with the remaining mint leaves.

MELE E PERE ARROSTO CON PROSCIUTTO

PROSCIUTTO WITH ROASTED APPLES AND PEARS

Cooking time: 25–30 minutes (including prep time)

Serves 4

4 small apples (about 300 g/10½ oz)
2 large Conference pears (about 400 g/14 oz)
2 rosemary sprigs
6 sage leaves
sea salt and freshly ground black pepper
extra-virgin olive oil
juice of 1 small lemon
20 g/¾ oz/2½ tbsp raw pistachio nuts
8 slices of prosciutto (Parma ham),
   about 125 g/4½ oz

Preheat the oven to 200°C fan/220°C/425°F/gas mark 7.

Wash the fruit. Slice the apples into fairly thick rounds and the pears lengthways into 4 quarters, discarding the pips. Place the fruit in a roasting tin (oven pan), sprinkle with the herbs, some salt and pepper, and drizzle with the olive oil and lemon juice. Roast in the hot oven for 15–20 minutes, until cooked through (but not falling apart) and golden.

Meanwhile, roast the pistachio nuts: spread them out on a baking tray (oven pan) and place in the hot oven for about 5 minutes; or toast in a frying pan (skillet) over a medium heat for about 3 minutes. Set aside to cool, then rub them between thumb and fingers to remove the skins.

Arrange the fruit on a serving dish with the slices of prosciutto, sprinkle with the skinned pistachio nuts, and serve.

SUSINE E FICHI AL FORNO CON PROSCIUTTO

CARAMELISED PLUMS AND FIGS WITH PROSCIUTTO

Cooking time: 20 minutes (including prep time)

Serves 4–6

4–6 large figs (about 240 g/8½ oz)
4 large plums (about 500 g/1 lb 2 oz)
4 thyme sprigs, leaves only
2 tbsp soft brown sugar
2 tbsp extra-virgin olive oil,
   plus extra for drizzling
juice of ½ lemon
sea salt and freshly ground black pepper
120 g/4¼ oz mixed baby salad leaves
25 g/1 oz/2½ tbsp walnuts, roughly chopped
8–12 slices of prosciutto

Preheat the oven to 210°C fan/230°C/455°F/gas mark 8.

Wash and dry the fruit. Slice the figs in half. Remove the stones (pits) from the plums and slice into segments. Place the fruit in an ovenproof dish, sprinkle with the thyme and sugar, and roast in the hot oven for 10 minutes. Remove from the oven and cool for about 5 minutes.

Meanwhile, combine the olive oil and lemon juice, season with some salt and pepper, and dress the salad leaves. Arrange the salad leaves on a large serving platter and top with the warm, caramelized fruit. Scatter over the chopped walnuts and the slices of prosciutto, then drizzle over a little more olive oil before serving.

SOUPS

Soups are simple to prepare, don't need a long time to cook and provide a nutritious, satisfying meal at any time. They are very versatile – depending on personal taste and the type of soup, they can be served either as they are, with chunky pieces of vegetables or other ingredients, or whizzed to a smooth, creamy consistency. They can also be prepared in advance and gently reheated to serve, or divided into portions and frozen for later. In fact, soups are so easy to prepare, it is often worth making more to put in the freezer, so that you always have a healthy meal to hand on those super-busy days or for when the cupboard is bare.

There is something so nourishing and feel-good about homemade soup that eating it always takes me back to my childhood, when we would very often have thick bean soups during the winter. We used to make them with dried pulses, which we always kept in our store cupboard, but these had to be soaked overnight and the cooking time was long. These days, we're lucky to have such a vast range of ready-to-use canned beans and pulses available to us; even vegetables can be bought pre-chopped, so you can have ready-prepared ingredients on hand to create delicious soups in no time.

In Italy, soup is usually served as a *primo* (starter) instead of pasta. Depending on when it is served, it could also be a filling bean-and-pasta soup for lunch, or a light broth for the evening meal. I hope you will enjoy making the super-simple soups in this book, which can be eaten both as starter or main course.

MINESTRONE VELOCE

QUICK MINESTRONE SOUP

Packed full of nutritious veggies, this soup is basically vitamins in a bowl! Based on the classic Italian minestrone, I have included borlotti beans and *pastina* (small pasta shapes). If you prefer, you could omit the *pastina*. In fact, you could omit any vegetable you don't like or don't have and replace with others. Most of these vegetables can be bought pre-washed and chopped, saving you time. For added flavour, you could serve with a dollop of Pesto Sauce (see p.184).

Cooking time: 35 minutes (not including veg prep)

Serves 4–6

4 tbsp extra-virgin olive oil
1 large onion, finely chopped
2 celery stalks, finely chopped
2 carrots, finely chopped
1 small fennel bulb, finely chopped
1 courgette (zucchini), cut into small chunks
1 large potato, peeled and cut into
    small chunks
280 g/10 oz Savoy cabbage, shredded
6 cherry tomatoes
a handful of fresh basil leaves
1.5 litres/52 fl oz/6½ cups vegetable stock
    (bouillon)
1 × 400-g/14-oz can of borlotti (cranberry)
    beans, drained
50 g/1¾ oz/⅓ cup frozen peas
75 g/2½ oz small pasta shells (pastina)
sea salt and freshly ground black pepper
grated Parmesan, to serve
Pesto sauce (see p.184), to serve (optional)

Heat the extra-virgin olive oil in a large heavy-based saucepan set over a medium–high heat. Add the onion and celery and sweat for a couple of minutes. Add the carrots, fennel, courgette, potato, cabbage, tomatoes and basil, and mix well. Pour in the stock, bring to the boil, then lower the heat and cook for 20 minutes. Add the borlotti beans, peas and pasta and continue to cook for about 6–8 minutes, until the pasta is cooked (check cooking times on the packet).

Remove from the heat, season with salt and pepper to taste, and serve with grated Parmesan and a dollop of pesto, if desired.

ZUPPA PICANTE DI CECI E BIETOLE

SPICY CHICKPEA AND CHARD SOUP

This is one of my favourite soups – I love chickpeas and I adore chilli! The chilli gives a real kick to the chickpeas and chard. I use one whole fresh red chilli in this recipe, but you can adjust according to taste. You could omit it altogether if you prefer or, if cooking for people who don't like spicy flavours, just add some dried chilli (hot red pepper) flakes over the top of individual portions at the end. If you can't find Swiss chard, you can substitute spinach, but add this about 5 minutes before the end of the cooking time. Served with toasted bread, this makes a delicious, warming meal.

Cooking time: 25 minutes (not including veg prep)

Serves 2 as a main course or 4 as a starter

1 tbsp extra-virgin olive oil
1 shallot, finely chopped
½ celery stalk, finely chopped
1 garlic clove, finely chopped
1 fresh red chilli, finely chopped
180 g/6¼ oz/2 cups Swiss chard, stalk and
   leaves finely chopped
200 g/7 oz canned chopped tomatoes
1 × 400-g/14-oz can of chickpeas (garbanzo
   beans) (240 g/8½ oz drained weight)
400 ml/14 fl oz/1¾ cups hot vegetable stock
   (bouillon)

To serve:
2–4 slices of country-style bread, such as
   Pugliese or a nice sourdough
1 garlic clove, peeled and left whole
extra-virgin olive oil, for drizzling

Heat the olive oil in a heavy-based saucepan set over a medium–high heat. Add the shallot, celery, garlic and chilli, and sweat for a couple of minutes. Stir in the Swiss chard and continue to sweat for 1 minute. Add the tomatoes, drained chickpeas and vegetable stock, bring to the boil, then lower the heat to medium, cover with a lid and simmer for 20 minutes.

Towards the end of the cooking time, grill (broil) or toast the slices of bread, rub the garlic clove all over the toasted surface of the bread, and drizzle with a little extra-virgin olive oil.

Divide the soup between individual bowls, drizzle with a little extra-virgin olive oil, and serve with the garlicky toasted bread.

ZUPPA DI FAGIOLI CANNELLINI CON PROSCIUTTO E SPINACI

CANNELLINI BEAN SOUP WITH PROSCIUTTO, SPINACH AND PARMESAN RIND

The delicate flavour of bay leaves and the slight saltiness of the prosciutto combine perfectly in this feel-good soup. Extremely quick and easy to prepare, it makes a satisfying complete meal served with some good bread, or an equally delicious starter. I have not added any salt, as the prosciutto and stock season the soup perfectly, but do check and add to taste, if necessary. For extra flavour, add some roughly chopped Parmesan rind, which is often added to soups in Italy. If you fancy an extra kick, sprinkle some dried chilli (hot red pepper) flakes in at the end.

Cooking time: 30 minutes

Serves 2 as a main course or 4 as a starter

2 tbsp extra-virgin olive oil
60 g/2¼ oz prosciutto (Parma ham),
   finely chopped
1 leek, finely chopped
1 small carrot, finely chopped
2 bay leaves
700 ml/24 fl oz/3 cups hot vegetable stock
   (bouillon)
a piece of Parmesan rind (about 20 g/¾ oz),
   roughly chopped
1 × 400-g/14-oz can of cannellini beans
   (240 g/8½ oz drained weight)
120 g/4¼ oz spinach leaves
freshly ground black pepper
freshly grated Parmesan, to serve (optional)

Heat the extra-virgin olive oil in a large heavy-based saucepan set over a high heat. Add the prosciutto and stir-fry for a couple of minutes, until almost crispy. Add the leek, carrot and bay leaves, then lower the heat to medium and sweat for about 4 minutes. Pour in the stock, add the Parmesan rind, and bring to the boil. Now, lower the heat, cover with a lid, and cook for 15 minutes, stirring from time to time with a wooden spoon, to prevent the Parmesan rind from sticking to the pan. Add the drained cannellini beans and spinach, season with some black pepper, and cook for a further 5 minutes.

Serve with a sprinkling of grated Parmesan, if desired.

ZUPPA DI FAVE AL TIMO CON PANCETTA
THYME-INFUSED BROAD BEAN SOUP, WITH CRISPY SMOKED PANCETTA

This is a delicious, creamy soup made using frozen broad (fava) beans. The subtle, smoky flavour of the pancetta really comes through and the crispy bits give a nice crunchiness to the dish. It is simply delicious at any time but would make a lovely starter for when you have guests over.

Cooking time: 25–30 minutes

Serves 4

20 g/¾ oz/1 generous tbsp butter
1 tbsp extra-virgin olive oil,
   plus an extra splash for frying
150 g/5½ oz smoked pancetta, finely chopped
1 onion, finely chopped
1 celery stalk, finely chopped
1 garlic clove, finely chopped
a handful of thyme leaves,
   plus a few to garnish
350 g/12 oz/2¾ cups frozen broad (fava) beans
1 large potato (about 200 g/7 oz), chopped
   into small cubes
1 litre/35 fl oz/4⅓ cups vegetable stock
   (bouillon)

Heat the butter and olive oil in a large, heavy-based saucepan set over a medium–high heat. Add a third of the pancetta, and all the onion, celery, garlic and thyme, and sweat for 5 minutes. Stir in the broad beans and potato, then pour in the stock, and bring to the boil. Reduce the heat, cover with a lid and simmer for about 10–12 minutes, until the beans and potatoes are cooked. Remove from the heat and allow to cool a little.

Meanwhile, add a splash of extra-virgin olive oil to a small frying pan (skillet) set over a medium heat. Add the remaining pancetta and stir-fry until nice and crispy. Set aside.

Transfer the slightly cooled soup to a blender or food processor and blend until smooth (you may need to do this in 2 batches). Return it to the saucepan and gently reheat, if necessary. Divide among individual bowls, sprinkle with the crispy pancetta and garnish with thyme leaves to serve.

ZUPPA DI FUNGHI

MUSHROOM SOUP

This simple mushroom soup delivers all the taste of wild mushrooms without the price tag! Reconstituted dried porcini are blended with vegetables and served with sautéed chestnut (cremini) mushrooms and pancetta. If you like, you could use a selection of wild fungi in season and, for vegetarians, omit the pancetta. Dried porcini are obtainable from all good Italian delis and larger supermarkets.

Cooking time: 25 minutes (including prep)

Serves 4

30 g/1 oz dried porcini
4 tbsp extra-virgin olive oil,
    plus extra for drizzling
1 large onion, finely chopped
1 celery stalk, finely chopped
1 large carrot, finely chopped
needles of 2 rosemary sprigs
2 garlic cloves, finely chopped
750 ml/26 fl oz/3¼ cups vegetable stock
    (bouillon)
20 g/¾ oz/4 tsp butter
50 g/1¾ oz pancetta, cubed
180 g/6¼ oz chestnut (cremini) mushrooms,
    sliced
sea salt, to taste

Place the dried porcini in a bowl, pour over warm water to cover, and leave to soften while you prepare the vegetables.

Heat 3 tbsp of the olive oil in a large saucepan set over a medium heat. Add the onion, celery, carrot, half the rosemary and half the garlic, and sweat for about 3 minutes. Drain the porcini (reserving the soaking water), roughly chop, add to the pan and continue to sweat for 2 minutes. Add the porcini soaking liquid and vegetable stock and simmer for 8 minutes.

Meanwhile, heat the butter and 1 tbsp of olive oil in a frying pan (skillet) set over a medium heat. Add the pancetta, the remaining rosemary and garlic, and sweat for 1 minute. Add the chestnut mushrooms, seasoning with some salt, and sauté for about 5–6 minutes, until the mushrooms are nicely browned all over.

Put the vegetables and stock into a food processor or blender and blend to a smooth consistency. Divide between 4 soup bowls, top with the sautéed mushrooms and pancetta, drizzle with a little olive oil and serve.

ZUPPA ALLA ZUCCA E PATATA DOLCE
SQUASH AND SWEET POTATO SOUP, WITH GARLIC AND ROSEMARY

Warming and comforting, this is my go-to soup during the autumn (fall) and winter, when squash is in season. You can use butternut or onion squash, or even pumpkin – it's your choice. I like the addition of sweet potato too, for its excellent nutritional value. Rosemary and chilli are good partners to all types of squash and sweet potato, but I have left the chilli optional (although when I make it, I like to add more chilli and make it nice and spicy!). Sometimes, when I am making this for the family, I omit the chilli during cooking and just add dried chilli (hot red pepper) flakes at the end to my portion.

This soup is really simple to prepare and takes no time to cook. The only part that takes a little time is the peeling and chopping of the squash. You can do this in advance, if you wish, and store the chunks in the fridge. You can also buy ready-peeled chunks of squash and sweet potato in supermarkets now!

Cooking time: 25–30 minutes (not including veg prep)

Serves 4–6

2 tbsp extra-virgin olive oil,
   plus extra for drizzling
3 garlic cloves, finely chopped
1 onion, finely chopped
2 rosemary sprigs, needles only
½ fresh red chilli (optional)
800 g/1 lb 12 oz squash, peeled and cut into
   chunks (weight after prep)
200 g/7 oz sweet potato, peeled and cut into
   chunks (weight after prep)
1.2 litres/40 fl oz/5 cups hot vegetable stock
   (bouillon)

Heat the olive oil in a large, heavy-based saucepan set over a medium heat. Add the garlic, onion, rosemary and chilli (if using) and sweat for about 4 minutes. Stir in the squash and sweet potato, then increase the heat and add the hot stock. Bring to the boil, then reduce the heat and cook for 12–15 minutes, until the squash and sweet potato are soft and cooked through. Remove from the heat and allow to cool a little.

Transfer the slightly cooled soup to a blender or food processor and blend until smooth (you may need to do this in 2 batches). Return the soup to the saucepan and gently reheat, if necessary. Divide between bowls and serve with a drizzle of extra-virgin olive oil.

CREMA DI FAGIOLI CON PESTO DI OLIVE

CREAMY BLACK-EYED BEAN SOUP WITH OLIVE PESTO

This is a delicious, creamy soup, which goes really well with the crunchy olive pesto. Make sure you get good-quality green olives, such as the Gaeta or Nocellara varieties (these, however, don't come ready-pitted, so you will have to do this yourself – you can easily do it while the soup is cooking). Quick and simple to prepare, this would make a lovely starter when you have guests or, of course, at any time.

Cooking time: 25 minutes (not including veg prep)

Serves 2–4

2 tbsp extra-virgin olive oil
1 shallot, finely chopped
½ leek, finely chopped
1 garlic clove, finely chopped
1 small carrot, finely chopped
½ small fennel bulb, finely chopped
leaves of 1 thyme sprig
1 × 400-g/14-oz can of black-eyed beans (peas), drained
600 ml/21 fl oz/generous 2½ cups vegetable stock (bouillon)
sea salt and freshly ground black pepper

For the pesto:
125 g/4½ oz/1¼ cups stoned (pitted) green olives
a handful of parsley
1 garlic clove
1 tsp capers
2 tbsp extra-virgin olive oil

Heat the olive oil in a large, heavy-based saucepan set over a medium heat. Add the shallot, leek, garlic, carrot, fennel and thyme, and sweat for about 4 minutes. Stir in the drained beans and cook for 1 minute to let the flavours infuse. Pour in the stock, increase the heat, and bring to the boil. Now reduce the heat, cover with a lid and cook for 15 minutes. Remove from the heat and allow to cool a little.

Meanwhile, make the pesto. Whiz all the ingredients in a food processor or blender, until well combined but retaining a crunchy texture. Set aside.

Transfer the slightly cooled soup to a blender or food processor and blend until smooth (you may need to do this in 2 batches). Return it to the saucepan and gently reheat, if necessary. Divide between individual bowls and serve with a generous dollop of the olive pesto.

ZUPPA DI PESCE VELOCE

QUICK FISH SOUP

This speedy soup is perfect for any fish lover who doesn't want to spend ages cleaning shellfish! Buy ready-peeled tiger prawns (jumbo shrimp) and ask your fishmonger to slice the squid and even chop the cod, if you're pressed for time. You can even buy the veggies ready-chopped too! This dish of delicate seafood, cooked in tomatoes and served with toasted bread, makes a delicious main course.

Cooking time: 20 minutes (not including prep)

Serves 4

4 tbsp extra-virgin olive oil,
    plus extra for drizzling
3 banana shallots, very finely chopped
2 celery stalks, very finely chopped
2 small carrots, very finely chopped
½ fresh red chilli, finely chopped
2 bay leaves
10 raw tiger prawns (jumbo shrimp)
200 g/7 oz squid, sliced into rings
200 g/7 oz cod, cut into small chunks
100 ml/3½ fl oz/7 tbsp white wine
600 g/1 lb 5 oz tomato passata
    (strained tomatoes)
sea salt, to taste
a handful fresh parsley, finely chopped
slices of toasted country-style bread, to serve

Heat the olive oil in a medium-sized, heavy-based saucepan set over a medium heat. Add the vegetables, chilli and bay leaves and sweat for about 2 minutes. Stir in the prawns and squid, and continue to cook for a further 3 minutes. Add the cod and cook for 1 minute. Pour in the white wine, increase the heat and cook off to evaporate. Carefully remove the cod chunks and set aside. Add the tomato passata, together with about 100 ml/3½ fl oz/7 tbsp of water and some salt to taste, lower the heat, then cover with a lid and cook for 10 minutes.

Return the cod to the pan and heat through for a final minute. Remove from the heat and serve sprinkled with the chopped parsley, a drizzle of extra-virgin olive oil, and with the toasted bread on the side.

PASTA

I don't think I know anyone who dislikes pasta. Universally loved, it is certainly a dish that Italians enjoy on a daily basis – for some, a meal would be incomplete without it!

Pasta is healthy, nutritious and versatile. It's so quick to cook – for me, pasta is 'fast food' at its best. Even the pasta sauces are uncomplicated and just as speedy to make. In fact, most of the sauces in this book are cooked while the pasta is boiling. You can also make some sauces in advance and freeze them for later. A simple, classic tomato sauce is worth making lots of and freezing it in batches for later use. On those weeknights, when time is really precious, you can rest assured that you have a good home-cooked meal at hand, which can be whipped up in no time at all.

Italians are passionate about their pasta and insist that only certain shapes go with certain sauces. Long pasta, such as spaghetti or linguine, tends to accompany light tomato or fish sauces. And short pasta shapes, such as penne or farfalle, go well with more robust-tasting, meaty sauces. It is for this reason that Italians keep a vast selection of pasta shapes in their store cupboards – when I visit my sister in Italy, I'm always amazed by how many different packets she has, and she lives by herself!

I like to keep both long and short shapes in my cupboard, as well as smaller shapes to add to soups. Spaghetti is a must in my store cupboard, because it is so easy to make a meal with, even when the fridge is bare. A simple sauce of *aglio, olio e peperoncino* (garlic, extra virgin olive oil and chilli) makes a quick meal at any time. For a milder flavour, my daughter Olivia's favourite is spaghetti with melted butter and Parmesan; it was always a winner when she was a toddler, and now, as a teen, she will often prepare it herself.

Pasta is also good for you. It is an ideal carbohydrate as it releases energy slowly, is easily digestible and its lack of fat makes it suitable for low-calorie diets (bearing in mind what goes into the sauce, of course!). You can be sure you are serving a good, nutritious meal made in no time.

MAFALDA CORTA CON SPINACI E MASCARPONE

CREAMY MASCARPONE AND SPINACH PASTA

For this quick and easy pasta dish, I have used a short-shaped pasta called *mafalda corta*, but you could substitute with farfalle or fusilli. The lemon zest added at the end gives the dish a lovely, fresh flavour.

Cooking time: 12–15 minutes

Serves 4

320 g/11¼ oz *mafalda corta* pasta
sea salt, for the cooking water
20 g/¾ oz/1 generous tbsp butter
1 garlic clove, slightly squashed
150 g/5½ oz baby spinach leaves
175 g/6 oz mascarpone
20 g/¾ oz/¼ cup grated Parmesan
freshly ground black pepper, to serve
zest of 1 small, unwaxed, organic lemon,
    to serve

Bring a large saucepan of salted water to the boil and cook the *mafalda corta* pasta for 8–10 minutes, until *al dente* (check the instructions on your packet).

Meanwhile, melt the butter in a large frying pan (skillet) over a medium heat, add the garlic and allow to infuse for 1 minute, stir in the spinach, cover with a lid, and cook for a couple of minutes, until the spinach has wilted. Discard the garlic.

In a bowl, combine the mascarpone and Parmesan, adding some salt and pepper to taste, until you obtain a creamy consistency. Add this to the cooked spinach and gently heat through.

Drain the pasta, reserving some of the cooking water. Add the pasta to the creamy spinach sauce, mixing well to combine, and adding a little of the cooking water, if necessary. Remove from the heat and serve with some freshly ground black pepper and a little grated lemon zest.

BUCATINI ALLA GRICIA
BUCATINI WITH PORK AND PECORINO

Along with its cousins, *carbonara*, *amatriciana* and *cacio e pepe*, this dish forms the backbone of Roman cooking. Using the typically favoured Roman ingredients of *guanciale* instead of pancetta, and Pecorino instead of Parmesan, this simple dish is often what locals cook when they need to make a quick meal. *Guanciale* is cured pork cheek – it has an intense flavour and is especially used in robust traditional Roman cuisine. It can be found in good Italian delis, and it can also be substituted with good-quality pancetta.

Cooking time: 15 minutes

Serves 4

320 g/11¼ oz *bucatini* pasta
sea salt, for the cooking water
200 g/7 oz *guanciale* or pancetta
2 tbsp extra-virgin olive oil
plenty of freshly ground black pepper
60 g/2¼ oz/1 scant cup grated Pecorino

Bring a large saucepan of salted water to the boil and cook the pasta until *al dente* (check the instructions on your packet for cooking time).

Meanwhile, chop the *guanciale* into small cubes or thin strips. Heat the olive oil in a frying pan (skillet) set over a medium heat, add the *guanciale* and stir-fry for a couple of minutes, until the pork is cooked through with a nice golden colour (be careful not to burn it!). Season with plenty of black pepper and add a ladle of the pasta cooking water, continuing to cook. When the pasta is ready, drain (reserving some of the cooking water) and add to the sauce. Mix well, then stir in the grated Pecorino and a little of the reserved pasta water, if necessary.

Serve immediately, with plenty of black pepper.

FARFALLE CON ASPARAGI E FUNGHI CON PANCETTA

FARFALLE PASTA WITH ASPARAGUS, MUSHROOMS AND CRISPY PANCETTA

Quick, nutritious and delicious, this pasta dish makes a substantial main course. If you're catering for vegetarians, just omit the crispy pancetta. For speed, buy ready-trimmed green beans, asparagus tips and ready-sliced mushrooms.

Cooking time: 20 minutes

Serves 4

240 g/8½ oz green (French) beans, trimmed
200 g/7 oz asparagus tips
400 g/14 oz farfalle pasta
120 g/4¼ oz pancetta or bacon slices
4 tbsp extra-virgin olive oil,
    plus extra for drizzling
2 large shallots, finely chopped
100 g/3½ oz mushrooms, thinly sliced
sea salt and freshly ground black pepper

Preheat the grill (broiler) to high.

Cook the green beans and asparagus in a saucepan of boiling water for about 5 minutes, until tender. Drain and set aside.

Bring a large saucepan of salted water to the boil and cook the *farfalle* pasta for 10–12 minutes, until *al dente* (check the instructions on your packet).

Meanwhile, place the pancetta or bacon slices under the hot grill, and cook on both sides until crispy, about 2–3 minutes per side. Set aside.

In a large frying pan (skillet) set over a medium heat, heat the olive oil, add the shallots, and sweat for a couple of minutes. Add the mushrooms and stir-fry for a minute or so. Add the cooked green beans and asparagus, some salt and pepper, to taste, a couple of tablespoons of the pasta's hot cooking water and cook for 2–3 minutes.

Drain the pasta, reserving a little of the cooking water. Add the pasta to the pan with the vegetables, turn the heat up to high and mix well to combine, adding a little of the pasta water to loosen the sauce, if necessary.

Serve garnished with the crispy pancetta, a grinding of black pepper and a drizzle of olive oil.

PENNE INTEGRALI CON BROCCOLI E PATATA DOLCE

WHOLEMEAL PENNE WITH BROCCOLI AND SWEET POTATO

Pasta with broccoli is a common dish in Italy, where it is usually flavoured with garlic and chilli. In this recipe, the broccoli is mashed in a blender and served with small chunks of delicious sweet potato, adding extra nutrients and colour to the dish. It makes a healthy combination, which goes really well with wholemeal (wholewheat) pasta. If you prefer, you can substitute the wholemeal penne with white-flour penne.

Cooking time: 20 minutes (not including prep)

Serves 4

320 g/11¼ oz wholemeal penne
400 g/14 oz broccoli florets
250 g/9 oz sweet potato, cut into cubes
sea salt, for the cooking water
3 tbsp extra-virgin olive oil,
    plus an extra splash
2 garlic cloves, finely chopped
½ fresh red chilli, finely chopped
60 g/2¼ oz/1 scant cup grated Parmesan, plus
    extra for sprinkling, if desired

Bring a large saucepan of salted water to the boil and add the pasta, broccoli and sweet potato. Cook until the broccoli is tender, 4–5 minutes. Remove the broccoli with a slotted spoon and set aside to drain in a colander. Continue to cook the pasta and sweet potato, until the pasta is *al dente*, 8–10 minutes (check the instructions on your packet).

Meanwhile, heat the olive oil in a large frying pan (skillet) over a medium heat, add the garlic and chilli, and sweat for about 30 seconds. Add the drained broccoli and stir-fry for 1 minute or so.

Remove from the heat and transfer the broccoli mixture to a food processor. Add a further splash of olive oil and the grated Parmesan and blend until smooth. Return the mixture to the frying pan.

Drain the pasta and sweet potato, reserving some of the cooking water. Add to the broccoli mixture, mix well and heat through, together with a little of the reserved cooking water, if needed.

Serve with an extra sprinkling of Parmesan, if desired.

LA PASTA AL PESCE DI MICHAEL
MICHAEL'S FISHY PASTA

This is my eldest son Michael's recipe – he often cooks quick dishes such as this. He was very excited when I told him of this book, as he is always looking for fast, nutritious meals to cook for himself and his partner, Sebastian, when they both return home after a long day's work. Served with perhaps a green side-salad, this wonderfully speedy and healthy dish is a complete meal.

Cooking time: 20 minutes

Serves 2 as a main course

sea salt
3 tbsp extra-virgin olive oil
1 large garlic clove, finely chopped
½ fresh red chilli, finely chopped
3 anchovy fillets
1 tsp salted capers, rinsed
1 × 400-g/14-oz can of plum tomatoes,
    drained, reserving 1 tbsp of the juice
150 g/5½ oz cod, skin-on, cut into 'fingers'
a handful of fresh parsley, roughly chopped
200 g/7 oz linguine

Place a large saucepan of salted water on the heat to boil.

In a large, deep frying pan (skillet), heat the olive oil over a medium heat, add the garlic, chilli and anchovy fillets and sweat for 1 minute or so, until the anchovy fillets melt. Stir in the capers, tomatoes, a quarter of the parsley, and some salt to taste, increase the heat and cook for 2 minutes. Add the cod pieces, skin-side down, reduce the heat to medium, add another quarter of the parsley, cover with a lid, and cook for 10 minutes. Remove the fish pieces and set aside.

When the pasta water has come to the boil, add the linguine and cook until *al dente* (check the instructions on your packet for cooking time). Drain, reserving a little of the cooking water.

Add the drained pasta to the tomato sauce and mix together, adding a little of the reserved cooking water, until well combined. Remove from the heat, stir in the remaining parsley, and serve with the pieces of cod on top.

CAVATELLI CON SALSICCA, FUNGHI E POMODORI SECCHI

CAVATELLI PASTA WITH SAUSAGE, MUSHROOMS AND SUN-DRIED TOMATOES

For this recipe, get the best Italian pork sausages you can (obtainable from Italian delis); both fennel- or garlic-infused sausages work well. Also, try to get good-quality sun-dried tomatoes, preferably ones which are not preserved in oil (also available at good Italian delis). If the tomatoes are in oil, then drain well, patting them dry with paper towels. *Cavatelli* are a small, hollow pasta shape from southern Italy, made from durum wheat semolina flour and water. This dish has all the flavours of rural Italy and makes a delicious complete meal.

Cooking time: 15 minutes (not including prep)

Serves 4

320 g/11¼ oz *cavatelli* pasta
sea salt, for the cooking water
4 tbsp extra-virgin olive oil
1 garlic clove, finely chopped
3 thyme sprigs
4 sun-dried tomatoes, finely chopped
350 g/12 oz Italian pork sausages, skinned
   and crumbled
100 ml/3½ fl oz/7 tbsp white wine
350 g/12 oz mushrooms, thinly sliced
40 g/1½ oz/generous ½ cup shaved Parmesan,
   to serve

Bring a large saucepan of salted water to the boil and cook the pasta until *al dente* (check the instructions on your packet for cooking time).

Meanwhile, heat the olive oil in a large frying pan (skillet) over a medium heat, add the garlic, 2 of the thyme sprigs and the sun-dried tomatoes, and sweat for 1 minute. Add the crumbled-up sausage meat and stir-fry for a few minutes, until lightly browned. Increase the heat to high, add the white wine and allow to cook off for a minute or so. Stir in the mushrooms and the remaining thyme sprig, then lower the heat, cover with a lid, and cook for 10 minutes. Add a little of the hot pasta water to stop it from drying up, if necessary.

Drain the pasta, reserving a little cooking water. Add the pasta and reserved water to the sausage and mushroom sauce, mix well to combine, and serve with shavings of Parmesan.

FUSILLI BUCATI CON PANNA, NOCI E BRICCIOLE CROCCANTI

FUSILLI BUCATI WITH WALNUTS, CREAM AND CRISPY CROUTONS

This creamy pasta dish goes really well with walnuts and celery. Do ensure you buy celery with lots of leaves and use the tender heart or the middle of the celery. In rural southern Italy, it was quite common to use breadcrumbs (from leftover bread) to top pasta dishes when cheese was unavailable, hence the idea of crispy croutons in this recipe. Quick and simple to prepare, this makes a deliciously different pasta dish.

Cooking time: 15 minutes (not including prep)

Serves 4

320 g/11¼ oz *fusilli bucati* pasta
1 garlic clove, peeled
60 g/2¼ oz day-old bread, cut into small cubes
1 celery heart with leaves, stalks thinly sliced
90 g/3¼ oz/⅔ cup walnuts
3 tbsp milk
a pinch of nutmeg
sea salt and freshly ground black pepper
100 ml/3½ fl oz/7 tbsp single (light) cream
1 tbsp extra-virgin olive oil

Bring a large saucepan of salted water to the boil and cook the pasta for 10–12 minutes, until *al dente* (check the instructions on your packet).

Meanwhile, place the garlic, 30 g/1 oz of the bread cubes, celery leaves, walnuts, milk, nutmeg, and some salt and pepper, to taste, in a food processor and whiz until smooth. Add the cream last and mix together. If the sauce is a little thick, add a little reserved pasta water. Set aside.

In a large frying pan (skillet), heat the olive oil over a medium heat. Add the sliced celery stalks and the remaining bread cubes and stir-fry for a minute or so, until golden.

Drain the pasta, reserving a little of the cooking water. Add the creamy sauce to a large saucepan set over a low heat and warm through. Add the pasta and reserved cooking water to the sauce and stir to combine. Divide between the plates and top with the crispy croutons and celery.

GNOCCHI CON GORGONZOLA E PERA

GNOCCHI WITH GORGONZOLA AND PEAR

Classic gnocchi and Gorgonzola are the perfect combination. The addition of sweet, ripe pears here really enhances the flavour, making this a delicious, speedy meal. Try to get good-quality gnocchi from an Italian deli; I really like the small variety, sometimes known as *chicchi*.

Cooking time: 10 minutes

Serves 4

3 tbsp butter
2 thyme sprigs, leaves only
1 ripe Conference pear, peeled and cut into
    small chunks
200 g/7 oz Gorgonzola, roughly chopped
5 tbsp milk
a pinch of grated nutmeg, plus extra to serve
500 g/1 lb 2 oz pack of ready-made gnocchi
sea salt, to taste

Place a large saucepan of water on the heat to boil.

In a large frying pan (skillet), melt the butter over a medium heat, add the thyme leaves and pear chunks and stir-fry for about 30 seconds. Stir in the Gorgonzola, add the milk and nutmeg, and stir well until the cheese melts. Turn the heat down to low.

When the water in the saucepan is boiling, drop in the gnocchi and cook for 1–2 minutes or so, until the gnocchi float to the top. At this point, use a slotted spoon to transfer the gnocchi into the creamy sauce and mix well to combine. Add a little salt to taste, remove from the heat, and serve immediately with a little extra grated nutmeg.

TROFIE AL PESTO CON NOCI E POMODORO

TROFIE WITH PESTO, WALNUTS AND TOMATO

Classic Ligurian *trofie al pesto* is now a popular pasta dish all over Italy and further afield. I remember when I first discovered *trofie* (short, thin, twisted eggless pasta) on a trip to the region in the 1990s – they were then unheard of in this country. I am pleased to say that, over the years, good Italian delis, and now some supermarkets, have started stocking it. *Trofie* take a little longer to cook than most other pasta shapes, so it's important to check the cooking instructions on your packet. I usually like to make my own pesto (see recipe on p.184), but you can find good-quality fresh pesto at Italian delis, as well as some excellent varieties in jars, which make great store-cupboard essentials. Here, the addition of walnuts and tomatoes makes this quick and simple dish a very tasty and nutritious meal.

Cooking time: 15–20 minutes (depending on pasta cooking time)

Serves 4

320 g/11¼ oz *trofie* pasta
sea salt, for the cooking water
100 g/3½ oz Pesto Sauce (see p.184)
a splash of extra-virgin olive oil
40 g/1½ oz/5 tbsp walnut pieces
2 tomatoes (about 250 g/9 oz), deseeded and
    roughly chopped
a few basil leaves, for garnish
grated Parmesan, to serve

Bring a large saucepan of salted water to the boil, add the *trofie* and cook for 12–15 minutes, until *al dente* (check the instructions on your packet).

Meanwhile, prepare the other ingredients.

When the pasta is nearly ready, place the pesto in a large frying pan (skillet) with a splash of extra-virgin olive oil and gently heat through. Drain the *trofie*, reserving a little cooking water. Add the *trofie* and reserved cooking water to the pesto sauce and mix well. Stir in the walnuts and tomatoes, remove from the heat and serve, garnished with basil leaves and some grated Parmesan, if desired.

CARBONARA DI SALMONE AFFUMICATO

SMOKED SALMON CARBONARA

This is a twist on classic carbonara, using smoked salmon instead of pancetta. You can buy smoked salmon trimmings, which are not only more economical but are already in small pieces, which saves on chopping time. Simple and nutritious, I'm sure this will become a favourite mid-week supper when time is precious! Although cheese doesn't really go with fish, I quite like a little grated Pecorino sprinkled on mine, but have left it optional.

Cooking time: 10 minutes (including prep!)

Serves 4

320 g/11¼ oz spaghetti or linguine
sea salt and freshly ground black pepper
2 egg yolks
1 tbsp milk
1 generous tbsp butter
3 tbsp extra-virgin olive oil
2 bay leaves
200 g/7 oz smoked salmon trimmings
3 tbsp white wine
a little grated Pecorino, to serve (optional)

Bring a large saucepan of salted water to the boil and cook the pasta until *al dente* (check the instructions on your packet for cooking time).

While the pasta is cooking, lightly beat the egg yolks in a bowl with the milk, and some salt and pepper, and set aside.

In a large frying pan (skillet), heat the butter and olive oil over a medium heat, add the bay leaves and sweat for 1 minute. Add the smoked salmon trimmings and stir-fry for a couple of minutes. Add the white wine and allow to cook off for a minute or so. Season with black pepper.

Drain the pasta, add to the frying pan with the smoked salmon and mix well. Remove from the heat, pour in the eggy mixture, and mix well to combine. Serve with a little grated Pecorino, if desired.

TAGLIOLINI CON PISELLI E RICOTTA

TAGLIOLINI PASTA WITH PEAS AND RICOTTA

A very simple dish of pasta with peas, with the added creaminess of ricotta, this makes a perfect, quick supper for all the family. You could substitute the *tagliolini*, which are like a thin version of tagliatelle, with linguine, or even use short pasta shapes such as farfalle. It's delicious either way.

Cooking time: 12–15 minutes

Serves 4

320 g/11¼ oz *tagliolini* pasta
sea salt, for the cooking water
2 tbsp extra-virgin olive oil
1 small onion, finely chopped
½ handful of basil leaves
200 g/7 oz/1½ cups frozen peas
200 ml/7 fl oz/scant 1 cup vegetable stock
   (bouillon)
250 g/9 oz ricotta
salt and freshly ground black pepper

Bring a large saucepan of salted water to the boil and cook the pasta until *al dente* (check the instructions on your packet for cooking time).

Meanwhile, heat the olive oil in a large frying pan (skillet) over a medium heat, add the onion and a couple of the basil leaves, and sweat for 2 minutes. Stir in the peas, the remaining basil leaves and vegetable stock, and cook for about 3 minutes, until the peas are tender.

In a bowl, combine the ricotta with a little freshly ground black pepper, and mash with a fork.

Drain the pasta, add to the peas, then stir in the ricotta, cooking for 1 minute or so, until nicely combined and heated through. Serve immediately.

LINGUINE CON ZUCCHINI E GAMBERETTI

LINGUINE WITH COURGETTES AND PRAWNS

Prawns (shrimp) and courgettes (zucchini) combine really well and, added to this speedy and simple pasta dish, makes a delicious, balanced meal. I like to grate courgettes – it's really quick and easy and you can do this while waiting for the pasta water to boil. However, to save more time, you can now buy them ready-spiralized and then give them a quick additional chop.

Cooking time: 20 minutes

Serves 4

400 g/14 oz linguine
sea salt
3 courgettes (zucchini), about 600 g/1 lb 5 oz/
    6 cups if buying ready-grated/spiralized
5 tbsp extra-virgin olive oil
3 garlic cloves, finely sliced
4 anchovy fillets
300 g/10½ oz prawns (shrimp), ready-peeled
a handful of basil leaves
juice of ½ lemon, to serve (optional)

Bring a large saucepan of salted water to the boil and cook the pasta until *al dente* (check the instructions on your packet for cooking time).

Meanwhile, grate the courgettes (if necessary) on the larger holes of a grater. Take handfuls of the grated courgette, squeeze out the excess water and set aside.

Heat the olive oil in a large frying pan (skillet) set over a low–medium heat. Add the garlic and anchovy fillets and sweat for 1 minute or so, until the anchovies have dissolved. Ensure that you do not burn the garlic, so lower the heat if necessary. Add the grated courgette and stir-fry for 2–3 minutes, until softened. Season with salt, to taste. Stir in the prawns and continue to cook for a further 2 minutes.

Drain the pasta, reserving a little of the cooking water, and add to the sauce in the pan, tossing together to combine. Stir in the basil and continue to cook for 1 minute, adding a little of the pasta cooking water if necessary. Serve immediately, with a squeeze of lemon juice to taste, if you like.

TROMPETTI CON CASTAGNE
TROMPETTI PASTA WITH CHESTNUTS

This is a simple, hearty pasta dish made with one of my favourite foods. I love chestnuts – every autumn (fall), I love to pick them and am quite happy to have a bowlful for dinner! Although chestnuts are easy to cook – I usually boil them with a bay leaf – you can find vacuum-packed, ready-cooked chestnuts in delis and good supermarkets. Once food for the poor, this versatile ingredient is now quite a delicacy, but it's so nutritious and combines really well with the creamy mascarpone here.

Cooking time: 20 minutes

Serves 4

360 g/12¾ oz *trompetti* pasta
4 tbsp extra-virgin olive oil
1 leek, finely chopped
80 g/2¾ oz pancetta, finely chopped
300 g/10½ oz cooked chestnuts,
    roughly chopped
2 rosemary sprigs, needles only
140 g/5 oz mascarpone
sea salt and freshly ground black pepper
grated Pecorino, to serve

Bring a large saucepan of salted water to the boil and cook the *trompetti* pasta for 10–12 minutes, until *al dente* (check the instructions on your packet).

Meanwhile, heat the olive oil in a large, deep frying pan (skillet) over a medium heat, add the leek and pancetta and sweat for a couple of minutes. Stir in the cooked chestnuts, the rosemary, and some salt and pepper, cover with the lid, and cook for 5 minutes.

In a bowl, combine the mascarpone with a little of the pasta's hot cooking water, to loosen it up a bit, and mix until creamy.

Drain the pasta, reserving a little of the cooking water. Add the pasta to the chestnut sauce, stir in the creamy mascarpone, and mix well, adding a little of the reserved cooking water, if necessary.

Serve with a sprinkling of grated Pecorino.

ORECCHIETTE CON SALSA AL POMODORO E RICOTTA SALATA

ORECCHIETTE PASTA WITH TOMATO AND RICOTTA SALATA

Ricotta salata is a hard version of the creamy cheese we are so familiar with; it is pressed, salted, dried and aged, and is perfect for grating over pasta dishes such as this one. *Orecchiette*, or 'little ears', is an eggless, handmade pasta from Puglia, which can be bought dried. If you don't want to make your own tomato sauce, or don't have any handy, buy a good-quality ready-made one. In fact, you can get all the ingredients for this recipe from a good Italian deli. Quick and easy to prepare, this dish is Italian simplicity at its best!

Cooking time: 15 minutes

Serves 4

400 g/14 oz *orecchiette* pasta
sea salt, for the cooking water
½ quantity Basic Tomato Sauce (see p.183)
80 g/2¾ oz *ricotta salata*, grated
a few basil leaves, to garnish

Bring a large saucepan of salted water to the boil and cook the *orecchiette* pasta for about 12 minutes, until *al dente* (check the instructions on your packet).

Meanwhile, in a large saucepan, gently heat through the tomato sauce.

Drain the pasta and toss through the tomato sauce. Divide between your serving bowls, sprinkle with the grated *ricotta salata* and garnish with basil leaves.

PASTA AL FORNO AI 4 FORMAGGI

MINI ITALIAN MAC 'N' CHEESE

This is the Italian way of preparing mac 'n' cheese, without the need to make a béchamel sauce. Quick and simple to prepare, it's a great way of using up leftover cheese. You can use a mixture of any cheeses you have in the fridge, which is great at Christmas time when you might have a lot. Served in individual ramekins, this nutritious, child-friendly dish will be everyone's midweek family favourite.

Cooking time: 15 minutes, including prep

Serves 4

butter, for greasing
320 g/11¼ oz pasta shapes, either *maccheroni*
    or *spirallini*
sea salt and freshly ground black pepper
70 g/2½ oz Emmental
80 g/2¾ oz Fontal (a type of Fontina cheese
    that is less oily when melted) or mature
    (sharp) Cheddar
100 g/3½ oz Gorgonzola
3 tbsp milk
40 g/1½ oz/generous ½ cup grated Parmesan,
    plus extra for sprinkling

Lightly grease 4 individual ramekin dishes with butter. Preheat the grill (broiler) to high.

Bring a large saucepan of salted water to the boil and cook the pasta for 10–12 minutes, until *al dente* (check the instructions on your packet).

Meanwhile, roughly chop the Emmental, Fontina and Gorgonzola cheeses, place in a large saucepan with the milk, and melt over a gentle heat, stirring with a wooden spoon, until you obtain a creamy consistency.

Drain the pasta and mix into the creamy cheese sauce, stirring in the grated Parmesan, and adding some salt and pepper, to taste. Divide between the ramekins, top with some extra grated Parmesan and place under the hot grill for 4–5 minutes, until golden-brown.

LASAGNE AL PANE CARASAU

TOMATO AND RICOTTA LASAGNE WITH PANE CARASAU

Sardinian *Pane Carasau* is more than just a simple flatbread and can be made into a variety of succulent dishes, such as this quick lasagne. Use the crispy bread as you would lasagne sheets; don't worry if it breaks -- you will need to break the sheets to fit your dish. This thin crispbread is not only quicker to cook than pasta sheets, but the result is a much lighter dish with all the flavour of a normal lasagne. If you don't have time to make your own tomato sauce or don't have any handy, just pick some up ready-made from a good Italian deli. The use of ricotta, much loved in southern Italian baked pasta dishes, makes a quick and light alternative to classic béchamel sauce.

Cooking time: 30 minutes (including prep)

Serves 4

250 g/9 oz ricotta
25 g/1 oz/⅓ cup grated Parmesan,
    plus extra for sprinkling
1 tbsp milk
sea salt and freshly ground black pepper
1 quantity of Basic Tomato Sauce (see p.183)
a handful of basil leaves
120 g/4¼ oz mozzarella, roughly chopped
120 g/4¼ oz *pane carasau* (from your local
    Italian deli)

Preheat the oven to 180°C fan/200°C/400°F/gas mark 6.

Combine the ricotta, Parmesan and milk, seasoning with some salt and pepper, and mix until creamy.

Line an ovenproof dish with a little of the tomato sauce. Top with a piece of *pane carasau*, followed by another layer of tomato sauce, then a layer of the ricotta mixture. Scatter over a few basil leaves and some of the mozzarella. Continue making layers like this, until you finish all the ingredients up, ending with a final layer of tomato sauce, scattered with some mozzarella and topped with a sprinkling of grated Parmesan. Bake in the hot oven for 15 minutes.

Meanwhile, heat the grill (broiler) to high.

Once baked, place the lasagne under the hot grill for about 3 minutes, until golden brown and bubbling.

RISOTTOS

In Italy, risotto has always been the staple food of the northern regions, where rice fields dominate the flat plains of the Po Valley. In traditional northern Italian families, a plate of risotto is served as a *primo* (starter) in place of pasta. It's strange – although I was brought up in the south, where pasta ruled, my mother would often cook a type of risotto with plenty of vegetables, especially on the days when she was busy and didn't have time to cook a lot.

Like pasta, risotto is nutritious, versatile, simple to prepare and quick to cook, often all in one pot! And, like pasta, if your cupboard is bare, a simple, basic risotto with butter and Parmesan makes nourishing comfort food. You can really add whatever ingredients you like to a risotto – my favourite is probably one with lots of veggies. The base of the risotto is usually made simply with a little finely chopped onion, and then I like to add whatever veggies I have – our family favourites are carrots and peas, which we always have in.

Risotto can also be made to impress, turning this humble grain into a meal fit for a king. Adding a little truffle butter or oil topped with shavings of truffle can be a real treat. Risotto rice goes so well with this highly prized fungus that in the regions of Italy where it is found – Piemonte, Umbria, Tuscany – it is quite normal to see this dish on the menus of local restaurants and trattorias.

The secret to a good risotto is the rice. Don't try to make risotto with any old rice because it just won't work. Try to buy the best you can afford – Italian delis will stock Carnaroli, Vialone Nano or a good Arborio. These short-grain varieties absorb liquid and release starch, making them ideal for creamy risottos. A good stock is important too, and I find a high-quality ready-made stock (bouillon) cube, or a 'stock pot' diluted in hot water, perfectly adequate. Once made, keep the stock hot by placing it in a pan over a low heat and gradually add a ladle or two at a time to the risotto, allowing the rice to absorb the liquid before adding more. Keep the heat under the risotto on low–medium and keep stirring all the time with a wooden spoon, to avoid the rice sticking to the bottom of the pan. Once cooked, take off the heat and beat in butter and Parmesan, if appropriate to the recipe, to give the risotto that extra creaminess.

RISOTTO CAPRESE

RISOTTO WITH TOMATO, MOZZARELLA AND BASIL

The ingredients for this risotto are taken from the classic *Caprese* salad – tomatoes, mozzarella and basil. Simple to make and extremely tasty, it's often my go-to midweek meal for the family.

Cooking time: 30 minutes

Serves 4

40 g/1½ oz/2 generous tbsp butter
2 tbsp extra-virgin olive oil
1 small onion, finely chopped
2 handfuls of basil leaves
260 g/9¼ oz cherry tomatoes, quartered
320 g/11¼ oz/1¾ cups risotto (Arborio) rice
100 ml/3½ fl oz/7 tbsp white wine
1.5 litres/52 fl oz/6½ cups hot vegetable stock
   (bouillon)
200 g/7 oz mozzarella, cut into small cubes
30 g/1 oz/⅓ cup grated Parmesan

Heat 20 g/¾ oz/1 generous tablespoon of butter and the olive oil in a large, heavy-based saucepan set over a medium heat. Add the onion and a couple of the basil leaves and sweat for 2 minutes. Stir in the tomatoes and continue to sweat for 1 minute. Stir in the rice, making sure each grain is coated in oil. Add the wine and cook until the rice has absorbed it. Then add a couple of ladles of hot stock, stirring with a wooden spoon until the rice has absorbed it all. Add a couple more ladles of stock and continue to cook in this way, stirring and adding more stock, for 17–20 minutes, until the risotto is cooked *al dente*.

Remove from the heat and add the remaining butter and mozzarella, stirring well until it has nicely melted into the risotto. Stir in the grated Parmesan and remaining basil leaves and serve immediately.

RISOTTO FESTIVO
CELEBRATION RISOTTO WITH PROSECCO, PRAWNS AND SCALLOPS

The perfect risotto for a special occasion! After you've added the prosecco into the risotto, have some glasses at the ready and share it among your guests. It's such an easy dish to make that you too can afford to indulge in a glass while cooking! When adding the butter at the end, known in Italian as *mantecare* ('to cook until creamy'), be careful not to mix too vigorously, to avoid the seafood breaking up. It won't affect the flavour, but it does look prettier to have the seafood whole when serving.

Cooking time: 30 minutes

Serves 4

40 g/1½ oz/2 generous tbsp butter,
    plus an extra knob (pat) to serve
2 tbsp extra-virgin olive oil,
    plus extra for drizzling
2 shallots, finely chopped
320 g/11¼ oz/1¾ cups risotto (Arborio) rice
125 ml/4 fl oz/½ cup prosecco
1.3 litres/44 fl oz/5½ cups hot vegetable stock
    (bouillon)
12 scallops
12 king prawns (jumbo shrimp)
a handful of fresh parsley, finely chopped

Heat the butter and olive oil in a large saucepan set over a medium heat. Add the shallots and sweat for 1 minute. Stir in the rice, making sure each grain is coated in oil. Add the prosecco, increase the heat and allow the alcohol to evaporate. Then add a couple of ladles of hot stock, stirring with a wooden spoon until the rice has absorbed it all. Add a couple more ladles of stock and continue to cook in this way, stirring and adding more stock, for 17–20 minutes, until the risotto is cooked *al dente*. About 5 minutes before the end of the cooking time, stir in the scallops and king prawns. Remove from the heat, mix in the extra knob of butter and the parsley, and serve with a drizzle of extra-virgin olive oil.

RISOTTO AI CALAMARI E ZAFFERANO

CALAMARI AND SAFFRON RISOTTO

This risotto makes a lovely meal at any time and the saffron gives it a nice yellow colour. The addition of lightly toasted pine nuts gives the dish a nice crunch, contrasting with the soft calamari (squid). I like to add a pinch of dried chilli (hot red pepper) flakes to mine, to give it an extra kick!

Cooking time: 25–30 minutes (not including prep)

Serves 4

4 tbsp extra-virgin olive oil,
   plus extra for drizzling
2 small shallots, finely chopped
400 g/14 oz calamari (squid), sliced into rings
320 g/11¼ oz/1¾ cups risotto (Arborio) rice
150 ml/5 fl oz/scant ⅔ cup white wine
1.5 litres/52 fl oz/6½ cups hot vegetable stock
   (bouillon)
a few saffron strands, diluted in a little of the
   vegetable stock
30 g/1 oz/2 tbsp butter
a handful of fresh parsley, finely chopped
50 g/1¾ oz/⅓ cup pine nuts (optional)
2 tsp dried chilli flakes (optional)

Heat the olive oil in a large, heavy-based saucepan set over a high heat, add the shallots and sweat for 1 minute, then add the calamari and stir-fry for 4 minutes. Stir in the rice, making sure each grain is coated in oil. Add the wine and cook until the rice has absorbed it. Reduce the heat to medium and add a couple of ladles of hot stock, stirring with a wooden spoon until the rice has absorbed it all. Add a couple more ladles of stock and continue to cook in this way, stirring and adding more stock, for about 20 minutes, until the rice is *al dente*.

Remove from the heat, add the diluted saffron strands, butter and parsley, and mix well.

Heat a small frying pan (skillet), add the pine nuts and cook for 1 minute or so until toasted.

Divide the risotto between 4 bowls, top with the toasted pine nuts and chilli flakes, if desired, and add a final drizzle of extra-virgin olive oil to serve.

RISOTTO AL ZAFFERANO CON PORCINI SECCHI

SAFFRON RISOTTO WITH DRIED PORCINI

This traditional Milanese classic, with the addition of dried porcini mushrooms, is delicious and a must for any mushroom lover. In season, you could make this dish with fresh porcini, but dried are so easily obtainable from Italian delis and supermarkets that I always keep a packet in my store cupboard.

Cooking time: 35 minutes

Serves 4

50 g/1¾ oz/⅓ cup dried porcini mushrooms
a couple of saffron strands
1 small onion
2 generous tbsp butter
2 tbsp extra-virgin olive oil
320 g/11¼ oz/1¾ cups risotto (Arborio) rice
100 ml/3½ oz/7 tbsp white wine
1.5 litres/52 fl oz/6½ cups hot vegetable stock
    (bouillon)
50 g/1¾ oz/¾ cup grated Parmesan, plus extra
    for serving

Soak the dried porcini and saffron strands in a little warm water and set aside for about 10 minutes, for the porcini to soften.

Meanwhile, finely chop the onion and prepare the other ingredients.

Heat 1 generous tbsp of butter and the olive oil in a medium, heavy-based saucepan set over a medium heat. Add the onion and sweat for a couple of minutes. Stir in the softened porcini (keep the soaking liquid) and stir-fry for 1 minute. Stir in the rice, making sure each grain is coated in oil. Add the white wine and the reserved porcini soaking liquid and cook, stirring with a wooden spoon, until the liquid has been absorbed by the rice. Add a couple of ladles of hot stock and cook, continuously stirring, until absorbed. Continue adding stock and cooking in this way for 17–20 minutes, until the risotto is cooked *al dente*.

Remove from the heat, mix in the remaining butter and grated Parmesan and serve immediately, with an extra grating of Parmesan, if desired.

RISOTTO DI CAROTA E SEDANO RAPA

CARROT AND CELERIAC RISOTTO

Carrot and celeriac is a match made in heaven and is one of my partner Liz's favourite food combinations. In fact, she came up with this idea for a risotto when we had some leftover celeriac and we have been making it ever since – we now purposely buy celeriac to make this dish! Grating the vegetables not only makes them quick to cook, but helps them mush nicely into the risotto. This makes a perfect one-pot meal for a mid-week family supper.

Cooking time: 30 minutes (not including veg prep)

Serves 4

50 g/1¾ oz/3½ tbsp butter
3 tbsp extra-virgin olive oil
1 small onion, finely chopped
2 carrots, peeled and grated
200 g/7 oz celeriac, peeled and grated
    (weight after prep)
340 g/11¾ oz/scant 2 cups risotto
    (Arborio) rice
100 ml/3½ fl oz/7 tbsp white wine
1.5 litres/52 fl oz/6½ cups hot vegetable stock
    (bouillon)
40 g/1½ oz/generous ½ cup grated Parmesan,
    plus extra for serving
a handful of parsley, finely chopped

Heat 25 g/1 oz/1½ tablespoons of butter and the olive oil in a large, heavy-based saucepan set over a medium heat. Add the onion, carrots and celeriac and sweat for 4–5 minutes. Stir in the rice, making sure each grain is coated in oil. Add the wine and cook until the rice has absorbed it. Then add a couple of ladles of hot stock, stirring with a wooden spoon until the rice has absorbed it all. Add a couple more ladles of stock and continue to cook in this way, stirring and adding more stock, for 17–20 minutes, until the risotto is cooked *al dente*.

Remove from the heat, add the remaining butter and Parmesan, and mix well with a wooden spoon. Stir in the parsley and serve immediately, with an extra sprinkling of Parmesan, if desired.

RISOTTO CON LENTICCHIE

LENTIL RISOTTO

This is a super, nutritious one-pot meal. Try to get Castelluccio lentils from Umbria, which should be available from good Italian delis. Not only do they cook quickly, but they taste delicious. If you can't get them, then use small brown or green lentils that don't require pre-soaking. If you are really pressed for time, use good-quality organic canned lentils, which, once drained, you can add about halfway through making the risotto.

Cooking time: 30–35 minutes

Serves 4–6

250 g/9 oz/1½ cups Castelluccio lentils
40 g/1½ oz/2 generous tbsp butter
1 tbsp extra-virgin olive oil
100 g/3½ oz pancetta, finely chopped
1 garlic clove, left whole
1 rosemary sprig
1 celery stick, finely chopped
1 carrot, finely chopped
100 g/3½ oz canned chopped tomatoes
250 g/9 oz/1½ cups risotto (Arborio) rice
1.5 litres/52 fl oz/6½ cups hot vegetable stock
    (bouillon)
30 g/1 oz/scant ½ cup grated Parmesan,
    plus extra for serving

Place the lentils in a saucepan, cover with water, bring to the boil and simmer for 10 minutes.

Meanwhile, heat 20 g/¾ oz/1 generous tablespoon of butter and the olive oil in a large, heavy-based saucepan set over a high heat. Add the pancetta and sauté for 2 minutes, then reduce the heat to medium, add the garlic, rosemary, celery and carrot and sweat for 4 minutes. Stir in the tomatoes and cook for about 3 minutes.

By this time the lentils should be cooked. Drain the lentils and add to the mixture in the pan. Stir in the rice, making sure each grain is coated in oil. Add a couple of ladles of hot stock, stirring with a wooden spoon until the rice has absorbed it all. Add a couple more ladles of stock and continue to cook in this way, stirring and adding more stock, for 17–20 minutes, until the rice is *al dente* and the lentils are cooked.

Remove from the heat, discard the garlic, if you like, then stir in the remaining butter and Parmesan. Serve immediately with extra grated Parmesan, if desired.

RISOTTO CON VONGOLE E PEPERONI MISTI

RISOTTO WITH CLAMS AND MIXED PEPPERS

For this recipe, I urge you to get the freshest and best clams you can; the liquid exuded from them gives the risotto its rich, delicious flavour. For speed, you can buy ready-sliced mixed peppers. The resulting dish is a colourful feast for the eyes and treat for the palate. A lovely dish to serve for a relaxed supper with friends, it is perfectly accompanied by a cold, crisp white wine such as a Greco di Tufo from Campania, or a Lugana from Lake Garda.

Cooking time: 35 minutes

Serves 4

1 kg/2 lb 4 oz clams
300 ml/10½ fl oz/1¼ cups white wine
1 garlic clove, left whole
a handful of parsley, finely chopped,
   with a few sprigs reserved whole
4 tbsp extra-virgin olive oil,
   plus extra for drizzling
2 banana shallots, finely chopped
400 g/14 oz mixed green, red and yellow
   (bell) peppers, thinly sliced
340 g/11¾ oz/scant 2 cups risotto
   (Arborio) rice
600 ml/21 fl oz/generous 2½ cups hot
   vegetable stock (bouillon)

Place the clams, 150 ml/5 fl oz/scant ⅔ cups white wine, garlic and a few whole sprigs of parsley into a large, heavy-based saucepan, cover with a lid and cook over a medium heat for 2–3 minutes, until the clam shells have opened.

Meanwhile, heat the olive oil in another large saucepan set over a medium heat, add the shallots and sweat for a couple of minutes. Increase the heat, add the peppers, and stir-fry for 3 minutes.

Drain the clams, reserving the cooking liquor, and set both aside. Discard any clams that have not opened.

Stir the rice into the pan with the peppers, making sure each grain is coated with oil. Add the remaining white wine and cook until it is absorbed. Add the liquor from the clams, reduce the heat to medium, and cook, stirring with a wooden spoon, until it has been absorbed. Add a couple of ladles of hot stock, stirring with a wooden spoon until the rice has absorbed it. Add a couple more ladles of stock and continue to cook in this way, stirring and adding more stock, for 17–20 minutes, until the rice is *al dente*.

At the end of the cooking time, stir in the clams. Serve immediately, with the finely chopped parsley and a drizzle of extra-virgin olive oil.

RISOTTO AI QUATTRO FORMAGGI

RISOTTO WITH 4 CHEESES

This has to be one of my favourite comfort foods. It's an ideal recipe to make when you have lots of pieces of leftover cheese in the fridge. The cheeses I have used are all typically Italian, but you can of course use whatever you have to hand – I find Cheddar is always such a perfect choice.

Cooking time: 25–30 minutes

Serves 4

50 g/1¾ oz/3½ tbsp butter
2 tbsp extra-virgin olive oil
1 small onion, finely chopped
350 g/12 oz/2 cups risotto (Arborio) rice
100 ml/3½ fl oz/7 tbsp white wine
1.5 litres/52 fl oz/6½ cups hot vegetable stock
    (bouillon)
50 g/1¾ oz Taleggio, roughly cut into small
    cubes
50 g/1¾ oz Dolcelatte, roughly cut into small
    cubes
50 g/1¾ oz/¾ cup grated Pecorino
50 g/1¾ oz/¾ cup grated Parmesan
a handful of fresh parsley, finely chopped
    (optional)

Heat 25 g/1 oz/1½ tablespoons of butter and the olive oil in a medium, heavy-based saucepan set over a medium heat. Add the onion and sweat for a couple of minutes. Stir in the rice, making sure each grain is coated in oil. Add the wine and cook until the rice has absorbed it. Then add a couple of ladles of hot stock, stirring with a wooden spoon, until the rice has absorbed it all. Add more stock and continue to cook in this way for 17–20 minutes, until the risotto is cooked *al dente*.

Remove from the heat, add the remaining butter and all the cheeses, and mix well until the Taleggio and Dolcelatte have nicely melted. Serve immediately, with a little chopped parsley, if desired.

RISOTTO CON SALSICCIA

SAUSAGE RISOTTO

This simple risotto makes a fantastic mid-week meal for all the family to enjoy. Ensure you get good-quality Italian pork sausages, available from good Italian delis. My favourite ones are the fennel-infused variety, but for a milder flavour go for *luganica* (a long, narrow sausage from northern Italy), or ask your deli to see what they have.

Cooking time: 30 minutes (not including prep)

Serves 4

40 g/1½ oz/2 generous tbsp butter
2 tbsp extra-virgin olive oil
1 small red onion, finely chopped
needles of 2 rosemary sprigs
300 g/10½ oz Italian pork sausages, skins
   removed and meat crumbled
325 g/11½ oz/1¾ cups risotto (Arborio) rice
100 ml/3½ oz/7 tbsp white wine
1.5 litres/52 fl oz/6½ cups hot vegetable stock
   (bouillon)
40 g/1½ oz/generous ½ cup grated Parmesan

Heat 20 g/¾ oz/1 generous tablespoon of butter and the olive oil in a large saucepan set over a medium heat. Add the onion and sweat for a minute or so, until softened. Add the rosemary and sausage meat, increase the heat to high, and stir-fry for 3–4 minutes, until sealed. Stir in the rice, making sure each grain is coated in oil. Add the wine and cook until the rice has absorbed it. Reduce the heat to medium, and add a couple of ladles of hot stock, stirring with a wooden spoon until the rice has absorbed it all. Add a couple more ladles of stock and continue to cook in this way, stirring and adding more stock, for 17–20 minutes, until the rice is *al dente*.

Remove from the heat, add the remaining butter and the Parmesan, mix well and serve at once.

FISH

Fish is extremely quick and easy to cook and really doesn't need too many ingredients or fancy ways of cooking. For me, the best fish is simply grilled or steamed and served with a drizzle of good extra-virgin olive oil and a squeeze of lemon. This is how most Italians enjoy fish, and as long as the fish is fresh, you can't go wrong.

I was lucky to have been born by the sea, where fresh fish was readily available, so it was not uncommon for us to eat it quite a few times a week. As we knew most of the fishermen in the area, I was often allowed to go with them and help out and, in return, they would give me local seafood to take home.

I love the markets in Italy with their fabulous displays of fresh fish. Whenever I'm home, I make sure I buy fresh anchovies and make *acciughe alla tortiera*, a very simple baked dish. I also preserve fresh anchovies in salt so that I can bring them home to England, to enjoy the taste of the sea all year round.

Fish is highly nutritious, low in fat and an excellent source of quality protein, vitamins and minerals. Scientific evidence suggests that eating fish a couple of times a week helps preserve mental agility and aids longevity. I remember my mother would make me eat fish eyes, which, when cooked, became little white, hard balls full of phosphorus. She said it was a nutrient that helped develop intelligence!

It's sad that a lot of fishmongers on the high street have closed in recent times. However, fish counters in supermarkets are now becoming increasingly adventurous, with monkfish, skate wings, gurnard, squid, fresh tuna, and more, making regular appearances alongside salmon and cod.

TONNO FRESCO CON VERDURE IN OLIO

FRESH TUNA WITH PRESERVED VEGETABLES

This is a perfect meal for a warm summer's evening. Fresh tuna is almost meat-like in texture, but still incredibly light. Good-quality preserved grilled vegetables are obtainable from your Italian deli counter. The crunch of the red onion perfectly complements this dish.

Cooking time: 10 minutes

Serves 4

160 g/5¾ oz preserved grilled courgettes
   (zucchini)
160 g/5¾ oz preserved grilled aubergines
   (eggplants)
1 small red onion, finely sliced
60 g/2¼ oz rocket (arugula)
120 g/4¼ oz baby plum tomatoes, sliced
12 basil leaves (optional)
450 g/1 lb fresh tuna, cut into chunks
30 g/1 oz/¼ cup pine nuts
4 tbsp extra-virgin olive oil, plus an extra
   splash for cooking
2 tbsp balsamic vinegar
sea salt and freshly ground black pepper

Arrange the preserved vegetables, red onion, rocket, tomatoes and basil leaves, if using, on a large serving dish.

Heat a griddle pan, or place a frying pan (skillet) over a medium heat with a splash of extra-virgin olive oil. Add the tuna chunks and cook for a couple of minutes on each side, until seared.

Top the vegetables on the serving platter with the seared tuna, sprinkle with pine nuts, drizzle with the extra-virgin olive oil and balsamic vinegar and season with some salt and pepper. Mix together well and serve.

SGOMBRI AL CARTOCCIO AL PROFUMO DI LIMONE

LEMON-INFUSED STEAM-BAKED MACKEREL

I love mackerel – not only is it a lovely fish, but it's nutritious and quick to cook. Cooking *al cartoccio* is an excellent way of keeping all the flavours intact in a healthy way. Serve the cooked mackerel in the foil, so that the delicious juices can be enjoyed with some good bread to mop them up.

Cooking time: 30 minutes (including prep)

Serves 2

2 mackerel (about 240 g/8½ oz each), heads
    removed (if desired) and cleaned
sea salt and freshly ground black pepper
2 rosemary sprigs
1 garlic clove, finely chopped
2 organic unwaxed lemons, finely sliced
extra-virgin olive oil

Preheat the oven to 180°C fan/200°C/400°F/gas mark 6.

Rinse the mackerel under cold running water, then pat dry well with paper towels. Place the fish on a large piece of parchment paper, which is in turn placed on top of a large piece of good-quality aluminium foil (you can place the fish on individual sheets or all in one package, as here). Place on a baking (oven) tray. Sprinkle salt and pepper all over the mackerel, including inside the cavity. Place a rosemary sprig inside each cavity, together with the garlic and half of the lemon slices. Top the mackerel with the remaining lemon slices, drizzle with olive oil, then wrap tightly in the foil and bake in the hot oven for 20 minutes.

To serve, place the whole parcel in the middle of the table and tuck in!

MERLUZZO CON PATATE ASSORTITE E AGRODOLCE DI CIPOLLA ROSSA

HAKE WITH MIXED POTATOES AND RED ONION AGRODOLCE

This lovely, delicate fish dish, enhanced by a selection of coloured potatoes and slight tangy onion *agrodolce*, makes a perfect main course when you're trying to impress! Chunks of hake are gently cooked with herbs and good extra-virgin olive oil, while a trio of potatoes are baking in the oven. Not only is it an attractive, vibrant dish, but both purple and sweet potatoes are highly nutritious with many health benefits.

Cooking time: 35–40 minutes (including prep)

Serves 4

a mixture of purple potatoes,
   sweet potatoes and white potatoes
   (780 g/1 lb 12 oz in total)
16 sage leaves
2 bay leaves
sea salt, to taste
6 tbsp extra-virgin olive oil,
   plus extra for drizzling
2 rosemary sprigs
1 tsp pink peppercorns
400 g/14 oz hake, cut into 4 chunks
½ red onion, very finely sliced
1 tsp capers
2 tsp white wine vinegar

Preheat the oven to 200°C fan/220°C/425°F/gas mark 7.

Wash the potatoes, dry them, then cut into halves or quarters depending on their size (keep the skins on). Add the chunks to a large saucepan filled with water and parboil for 10 minutes. Drain well, place in a roasting dish with 8 sage leaves and the bay leaves, sprinkle with some salt and drizzle with a little olive oil. Bake in the hot oven for about 15–20 minutes, until cooked through and beginning to colour.

Meanwhile, in a pan large enough to fit the fish chunks, add the olive oil, the remaining sage, rosemary and pink peppercorns, and cook over a gentle heat for a minute or so, to allow the herbs to infuse. When the olive oil begins to bubble slightly, add the hake chunks, cover with a lid and continue to cook over a low heat for 15 minutes, carefully turning the fish over halfway through.

Meanwhile, to make the *agrodolce*, combine the red onion, capers and white wine vinegar in a small dish.

Arrange the potatoes and fish on a large serving dish. Alternatively, divide between individual plates, making sure everyone gets a selection of coloured potatoes. Drizzle the herby cooking juices from the pan over the top, followed by the onion *agrodolce*.

SOGLIOLA CON SPECK E CIPOLOTTI

FILLETS OF SOLE WITH SPECK AND CIPOLOTTI ONIONS

Sole is a light, delicate fish that marries really well with the slight smoky aroma of speck, a cured ham from north-east Italy. Speck is obtainable from good Italian delis, but if you prefer, you could substitute it for the slightly blander-tasting prosciutto. *Cipolotti* are a large version of spring onions (scallions), which you can get in some greengrocers; otherwise, buy the largest spring onions you can find or substitute with shallots or leeks. A quick and simple dish, this makes a lovely and impressive main course, especially when you have guests round.

Cooking time: 25–30 minutes (including prep)

Serves 2–4

250 g/9 oz skinless sole fillets
sea salt and freshly ground black pepper
4 slices of speck
1 generous tbsp butter
2 tbsp extra-virgin olive oil
150 g/5½ oz *cipolotti* onions, trimmed and
   sliced in half
80 ml/2½ fl oz/5 tbsp white wine

Slice the sole fillets in half lengthways and season lightly all over with salt and pepper. Lay the speck slices on a board, place a sole fillet on top of each and roll up. Set aside.

In a large frying pan (skillet) set over a high heat, melt the butter and 1 tablespoon of the olive oil, add the *cipolotti* and sweat for 1 minute. Add 50 ml/1½ fl oz/3 tablespoons of the wine, cover with a lid, reduce the heat to medium and cook for 4–5 minutes, until the *cipolotti* are just tender. Remove the *cipolotti* from the pan and keep warm.

Place the remaining olive oil in the pan, add the wrapped sole fillets, cover with a lid, and cook over a medium heat for 10 minutes, carefully turning them over halfway through. Increase the heat, add the remaining wine and allow to cook off. Remove from the heat and serve immediately with the *cipolotti*.

FILETTI DI TROTA ALLA VENDEMIA

BAKED TROUT AND GRAPES WITH A RED WINE SAUCE

The Italian title of this dish suggests harvest time and a dish such as this would be cooked in rural wine-making areas using meat rather than fish. However, I find earthy-tasting fillets of trout work just as well and the combination of slightly crunchy veg, soft sweet-tasting grapes and the slightly bitter wine sauce go really well together. Don't worry if you find the wine sauce too bitter on tasting – eating it together with the fish will change your mind!

Cooking time: 30 minutes (not including veg prep)

Serves 4

4 trout fillets (about 150 g/5½ oz each)
sea salt and freshly ground black pepper
50 g/1¾ oz/generous 3 tbsp butter
1 onion, thinly sliced
2 celery stalks, thinly sliced
1 large carrot, sliced into thin batons
2 bay leaves
2 thyme sprigs
200 g/7 oz white grapes
200 g/7 oz red grapes
30 g/1 oz/¼ cup pine nuts
20 g/¾ oz/2½ tbsp plain (all-purpose) flour
300 ml/10½ fl oz/1¼ cups red wine

Preheat the oven to 160°C fan/180°C/350°F/gas mark 4.

Place the trout fillets in an ovenproof dish and season with a little salt and pepper.

Melt 30 g/1 oz/2 tbsp of the butter in a frying pan (skillet) set over a medium heat. Add the vegetables, herbs and grapes and sweat for 3 minutes. Pour over the fish, sprinkle with pine nuts, cover with foil, and cook in the hot oven for 20 minutes.

Meanwhile, prepare the sauce. Melt the remaining 20 g/¾ oz/generous 1 tbsp butter in a small saucepan set over a medium heat. Remove from the heat and whisk in the flour, mixing well to avoid lumps. Add a couple of tablespoons of the red wine and continue to whisk. Place back over the heat, gradually add all the wine, whisking all the time, and cook until the sauce has thickened.

Remove the fish from the oven, carefully divide between the plates and serve with the wine sauce.

BRANZINO CON FUNGHI
SEABASS WITH FORESTIERE MUSHROOMS

When I originally set out to make this recipe, I wanted to use porcini mushrooms; however, I was testing out of season and porcini were unavailable. I found a type of cultivated mushroom called *Forestiere,* which looks similar to large, brown chestnut mushrooms. The mushroom has a slightly wild, forest-y taste and works really well with the seabass. If you can't find this type, any cultivated brown or white mushroom is fine, and, of course, if you can get porcini during the autumn (fall), then this quick, simple dish will be a real treat! Serve with some boiled new potatoes for a delicious meal.

Cooking time: 15 minutes (not including prep)

Serves 4

3 tbsp extra-virgin olive oil,
    plus an extra splash
2 garlic cloves, finely chopped
150 g/5½ oz *Forestiere* mushrooms,
    thinly sliced
sea salt and freshly ground black pepper
240 g/8½ oz cherry tomatoes, halved
a handful of fresh parsley, roughly chopped
30 g/1 oz/2 tbsp butter
4 seabass fillets (about 125 g/4½ oz each)

Heat the olive oil in a frying pan (skillet), add the garlic and sweat over a medium heat for 1 minute. Add the mushrooms, season with some salt and pepper and stir-fry for 1 minute. Remove the mushrooms and set aside.

In the same pan, add the tomatoes with another splash of olive oil, and stir-fry for 2 minutes. Return the mushrooms to the pan and continue to cook for a further 2 minutes. Stir in the parsley and turn off the heat.

Meanwhile, in another, larger frying pan, melt the butter, add the fish skin-side down, season with some salt and pepper and fry over a medium heat for 5 minutes. Turn the fish over carefully and cook for a further 2 minutes, until cooked through.

Serve the fish with the mushroom mixture.

FILETTI DI PLATESSA CON BURRO, LIMONE E CAPPERI

PLAICE FILLETS WITH BUTTER, LEMON AND CAPERS, SERVED WITH BABY POTATOES

I had never heard of plaice until I came to England and found it on menus at fish and chip shops. In Italy, anchovies and capers are often added to fish dishes, so I wanted to incorporate these Italian ingredients with this very English fish. The combination of capers and lemon juice is a winner and gives a delicious kick to the dish. Be careful not to add too much salt to the fish, because anchovies and capers are quite salty. Served with minty, boiled baby potatoes, this makes a lovely, light and nutritious meal, perfect for both a quick and easy mid-week supper as well as for entertaining. I love to mop up the buttery lemon sauce with some good bread at the end!

Cooking time: 15–20 minutes (including prep)

Serves 2–4

500 g/1 lb 2 oz baby potatoes,
    washed and scrubbed
4 plaice fillets (about 180 g/6¼ oz each)
sea salt
90 g/3¼ oz/6 tbsp butter, plus an extra knob
    (pat) for the potatoes
2 anchovy fillets, finely chopped
2 tbsp capers in brine (if under salt, ensure
    you wash salt completely off)
juice of 1 large organic unwaxed lemon
1 tbsp chopped fresh parsley
a handful of fresh mint, finely chopped

Place the baby potatoes in a large saucepan of water, bring to the boil and cook for about 10 minutes, until the potatoes are tender.

Meanwhile, season the fish with very little salt. Heat 30 g/1 oz/2 tablespoons of the butter in a large frying pan (skillet) set over a medium heat. Add the anchovy fillets and sauté for a couple of minutes until the anchovies dissolve. Holding the plaice fillets with your fingertips, dip both sides into the buttery mixture, before placing each fillet skin-side down into the pan. Add the capers, half the lemon juice, a further 30 g/1 oz/2 tablespoons of butter and the parsley, and cook for 2–3 minutes, until the fish is cooked through. Remove the fish to a serving dish and set aside. Increase the heat, add the remaining butter to the pan, stirring well until melted, then remove from the heat and pour over the fish, together with the remaining lemon juice.

Drain the potatoes, toss with some butter and the mint, and serve immediately with the fish.

CALAMARI ALLE OLIVE

SQUID WITH OLIVES

A traditional southern Italian dish which is perfect to enjoy with a group of friends for a casual
supper. Serve with lots of toasted country-style bread to mop up the tomato sauce.

Cooking time: 25 minutes

Serves 4–6

1 kg/2 lb 4 oz squid
4 tbsp extra-virgin olive oil
2 banana shallots, finely chopped
2 garlic cloves, finely chopped
a handful of fresh parsley, finely chopped
sea salt and freshly ground black pepper
100 ml/3½ fl oz/7 tbsp white wine
240 g/8½ oz tomato passata (strained
    tomatoes)
200 g/7 oz black olives
toasted country-style bread, to serve

Wash the squid under cold running water, pat dry on paper towels and cut into rings.

Heat the olive oil in a large saucepan set over a medium heat. Add the shallots, garlic and
parsley and sweat for a couple of minutes. Stir in the squid rings, season with a little salt
and pepper, increase the heat to high and stir-fry for 1 minute. Add the white wine and allow
the alcohol to cook off. Add the tomato passata and olives, cover with a lid, reduce the heat to
medium and cook for 15 minutes. Serve at once with the bread on the side.

SALMONE CON FINOCCHIO
SALMON WITH FENNEL

Salmon and fennel go well together and the addition of the creamy sauce makes this a very tasty meal, which can be made in no time. As the salmon is coated in flour and fried, it retains a slight crispiness on the outside, which combines perfectly with the slightly crunchy fennel.

Cooking time: 30 minutes (including prep)

Serves 4

2 fennel bulbs
zest and juice of 1 lemon
4 salmon fillets (about 110 g/3¾ oz each)
sea salt and freshly ground black pepper
plain (all-purpose) flour, for coating
80 g/2¾ oz/5½ tbsp butter
a splash of white wine
100 ml/3½ fl oz/7 tbsp whipping cream
30 g/1 oz/⅓ cup grated Parmesan

Preheat the oven to 200°C fan/220°C/425°F/gas mark 7.

Remove the green fronds from the fennel bulb and set aside. Slice each bulb into 8 segments, place into acidulated water (water mixed with the lemon juice) and set aside.

Cut each salmon fillet into 4 chunks, sprinkle with salt and pepper, and coat in flour. Heat 40 g/1½ oz/2 generous tablespoons of the butter in a frying pan (skillet) set over a medium heat. Add the salmon chunks and seal on both sides, for about 3–4 minutes. Add a splash of white wine and cook for a further minute. Remove the salmon and set aside.

In the same pan, heat the remaining butter, add the fennel segments and some salt and pepper, and cook on a medium–high heat for a couple of minutes on both sides.

Combine the cream, Parmesan and lemon zest and season with some more salt and pepper.

Arrange the fennel in an ovenproof dish, place the salmon chunks on top and pour over the creamy mixture. Bake in the hot oven for 5 minutes, until golden. Serve, sprinkled with the reserved fennel fronds.

PESCATRICE IN PADELLA CON SALSA DI ALLORO

PAN-FRIED MONKFISH WITH A BAY LEAF AND SHALLOT SAUCE

This dish is quick and simple to prepare; while the monkfish is cooking, you can get on with making the sauce at the same time. I like to serve this dish with lots of good crusty bread to mop up the sauce. Make sure you use a good-quality dry, crisp white wine, otherwise you could get a bitter aftertaste. If you prefer, you can substitute the monkfish with cod or hake.

Cooking time: 20 minutes

Serves 2–4

2 monkfish tails (about 650 g/1 lb 7 oz in total)
sea salt and freshly ground black pepper
5 tbsp extra-virgin olive oil
3 anchovy fillets

For the sauce:
1 tsp cornflour (cornstarch)
350 ml/12 fl oz/1½ cups white wine
8 tbsp extra-virgin olive oil
8 bay leaves, finely chopped
2 shallots, finely chopped
2 garlic cloves, finely chopped
a handful of parsley, finely chopped

Cut each monkfish tail in half, so that you have 4 pieces of fish, and season with a little salt and pepper.

Heat 5 tablespoons of olive oil in a frying pan (skillet) set over a medium heat. Add the anchovies and cook until dissolved. Add the monkfish and cook for 5 minutes on each side.

Meanwhile, blend the cornflour with the white wine and set aside. In a small saucepan set over a medium heat, heat the 8 tablespoons of olive oil, add the bay leaves, shallots and garlic and sweat for about 4 minutes. Stir in the parsley, add the white wine mixture, increase the heat and cook for 5–6 minutes, until the sauce thickens. Remove from the heat, season with salt and pepper, and serve with the monkfish.

RAZZA CON POMODORINI, AGLIO E BASILICO

SKATE WITH CHERRY TOMATOES, GARLIC AND BASIL

I love skate – whenever I see it at the fishmonger I have to buy it and usually cook it in this simple, very southern-Italian way. Served with slices of toasted country bread, it makes a substantial meal for two, although if you are serving other food, you could stretch it to three servings. You can serve the sauce with linguine or spaghetti as a starter and enjoy the fish as a main course – this is quite common in Italy. If you do this, add the cooked pasta at the end when the sauce is reducing.

Cooking time: 20 minutes (including prep)

Serves 2

1 large skate wing (about 500 g/1 lb 2 oz)
sea salt and freshly ground black pepper
6 tbsp extra-virgin olive oil
4 garlic cloves, finely sliced
¼ fresh red chilli, finely chopped
2 tsp capers
400 g/14 oz baby plum tomatoes, halved
250 ml/9 fl oz/1 generous cup freshly boiled
   water
2 tbsp white wine
a handful of basil leaves
2–4 slices of sourdough bread, toasted

Season the skate all over with salt and pepper.

In a frying pan (skillet) large enough to accommodate the skate (if necessary, slice the fish to fit the pan), heat the olive oil over a medium heat. Add the garlic, chilli and capers and sweat for about 30 seconds, then add the tomatoes and cook for a further 30 seconds. Add the hot water, wine, basil and some salt and cook for 3 minutes. Add the skate, cover the pan with a lid and cook for 10–12 minutes, until the fish is cooked through. Carefully turn the skate over halfway through the cooking time.

Carefully remove the fish from the pan and place on a serving dish. Increase the heat to high and cook the tomato sauce for a couple of minutes, until it has reduced slightly. Remove from the heat, pour the sauce over the fish and serve with slices of toasted sourdough bread.

MEAT

When it comes to meat, one of my guilty pleasures is a nice, juicy, medium-rare steak *ai ferri,* which means grilled or griddled without adding any fat. Quick and simple to prepare, it takes no time to cook and, together with a mixed salad and some bread, it is a feast for a king!

When buying meat that requires little cooking time, I cannot stress enough the importance of getting the best, organic, ethically sourced meat you can afford. Good-quality meat is an excellent source of protein, but you don't have to eat it every day. I find I am going back to my childhood days when we really only had meat on Sundays and feast days, but it was always good-quality and more often than not we knew the farmer. So not only did we know where our meat came from, but it was always full of flavour and needed little seasoning.

In Italy, a small piece of meat is usually served as a main course after the obligatory *primo* of pasta, risotto or soup. Popular everyday meat dishes, such as *scaloppine* of veal or pork, are quickly pan-fried in butter and served with a squeeze of lemon. In fact, it is not uncommon to have lemon wedges served alongside most fried or grilled meats in Italy.

Cotoletta impanatta is another popular quick meal, comprising thin slices of either veal, pork, chicken or turkey, coated in breadcrumbs and shallow-fried. It is often enjoyed by children, but adults love it too! *La bistecca* (steak) is an all-time favourite and cooking slices of meat *alle brace* (on the barbecue) is popular during summer or when you have a crowd.

SALTIMBOCCA DI POLLO
CHICKEN SALTIMBOCCA WITH FONTINA, PROSCIUTTO AND SAGE

Named for its irresistible taste – saltimbocca literally translates as 'jump in the mouth' – this classic Roman speciality has become a popular meat dish all over the world. Originally made with veal, it can also be made with pork or chicken. Don't season the chicken, as you get saltiness from the prosciutto and tasty deliciousness from the sage and oozing Fontina. Serve with boiled potatoes and steamed greens for a delicious lunch or dinner.

Cooking time: 15 minutes (if chicken is already sliced)

Serves 4

350 g/12 oz chicken breast, thinly sliced to
    obtain 8 slices (you can ask your butcher
    to do this for you)
8 large sage leaves
50 g/1¾ oz Fontina, cut into 8 thin slices
8 slices of prosciutto (Parma ham),
    about 125 g/4½ oz
50 g/1¾ oz/3 tbsp butter
50 ml/1½ fl oz/3 tbsp white wine

Place the chicken slices on a board (the slices should be no more than 5-mm/¼-in thick – if necessary, flatten with a meat mallet). Place a sage leaf in the middle of each one, followed by a slice of Fontina and top with a slice of prosciutto, making sure the prosciutto covers the cheese. If your chicken slices are small, fold the prosciutto so that you have a double layer. Secure the ingredients in place with cocktail sticks (toothpicks) to ensure nothing falls off.

Melt 30 g/1 oz/2 tbsp of the butter in a large frying pan (skillet) set over a medium heat. Add the *saltimbocca*, chicken-side down, and cook for 2 minutes, or until sealed. Turn them over and cook for a further 2 minutes. Turn them over again, increase the heat to high, add the white wine and cook for 1 minute. Remove the chicken and place on a serving dish. Add the remaining butter to the frying pan and cook for about 30 seconds, until creamy. Pour the buttery sauce over the chicken and serve immediately.

COSTOLLETTE DI AGNELLO ALL'ACCIUGA

ANCHOVY-INFUSED LAMB CUTLETS

Lamb and anchovy is a match made in heaven, especially in this quick and simple dish using cutlets. You can use cutlets that are on or off the bone, so the weight may vary. This dish makes a great mid-week supper, but is also perfect for a more formal meal when you have guests. It is delicious served with couscous or with some good bread to mop up the juices.

Cooking time: 25 minutes

Serves 4

8 lamb cutlets (about 800 g/1 lb 12 oz in total)
3 tbsp extra-virgin olive oil
80 ml/2½ fl oz/5 tbsp white wine
2 garlic cloves, finely sliced
needles of 2 rosemary sprigs
leaves of 2 thyme sprigs
7 anchovy fillets
2 tbsp white wine vinegar

Place the lamb in a dish, drizzle with 1 tbsp of olive oil, pour over the wine and scatter over the garlic and herbs. Set aside for 15 minutes for the flavours to infuse.

In a large frying pan (skillet) set over a medium heat, heat the remaining olive oil, add the anchovy fillets, and gently cook until the anchovy fillets dissolve. Increase the heat, add the lamb cutlets, and cook to seal well on both sides. Add the lamb marinade, cover with a lid, reduce the heat to medium, and cook for about 5 minutes, turning the lamb cutlets over from time to time.

Remove the lamb and place on a serving dish. Stir the vinegar into the sauce in the pan over a medium heat, pour over the lamb and serve.

COTOLETTE DI MAIALE RIPIENE DI SOTT'OLI

PORK STEAKS IN BREADCRUMBS WITH A PRESERVED VEGETABLE FILLING

Meat coated in breadcrumbs is always a popular meal in my house, especially among the children. To give the pork steaks a bit of a kick, my sister Adriana came up with the idea of filling them with some of my home-preserved vegetables. To prevent the filling from escaping, the meat has been double-dipped in egg and double-coated in breadcrumbs – this also gives it a crispier texture, which makes it all the more tasty. This is delicious served with the Oregano-Infused Mixed Tomato Salad (see p.28) and lemon wedges, if desired, and can also be enjoyed cold in-between some bread for a yummy sandwich.

Cooking time: 25 minutes (including prep)

Serves 4

4 pork steaks (about 500 g/1 lb 2 oz in total)
180 g/6¼ oz preserved artichokes, drained
    weight, very finely chopped
6 sun-dried tomatoes preserved in oil,
    very finely chopped
8 black olives, very finely chopped
4 eggs
10 g/¼ oz/5 tbsp grated Parmesan
sea salt and freshly ground black pepper
320 g/11¼ oz breadcrumbs
60 g/2¼ oz/4 tbsp butter
8 tbsp sunflower oil
lemon wedges, to serve (optional)

Slice the pork steaks horizontally in half, so you have 8 thin slices, lay them out flat on a board and flatten each one out with a meat mallet, to make them as thin as you can. Alternatively, you could ask your butcher to do this, to save time.

Top 4 of the slices of pork with the chopped artichokes, sun-dried tomatoes and olives, then sandwich together with the other slices of pork, pressing down well.

Beat the eggs lightly in a bowl and combine with the grated Parmesan, seasoning with some salt and pepper. Place the breadcrumbs on a shallow plate. Carefully dip the filled pork steaks first in the eggy mixture, then coat in the breadcrumbs. Repeat this one more time, so that all the steaks have a double coating.

Heat the butter and oil in a large frying pan (skillet) set over a medium–high heat and fry the filled pork steaks for about 5 minutes on each side. Remove and place on paper towels to drain off any excess oil. Serve with lemon wedges and a tomato salad.

FEGATO CON CIPOLLE E UVETTA CON POLENTA SVELTA

CALVES' LIVER WITH ONIONS AND SULTANAS, SERVED WITH QUICK POLENTA

I love calves' liver! It is so good for you, without the fat that most other cuts of meat contain. It is also extremely quick to cook and makes a tasty nutritious meal. This is my version of the classic *Fegato alla Veneziana,* where onions are steam-fried over a gentle heat until transparent and softened. The addition of sultanas (golden raisins) here adds a pleasant sweetness. If you can't find calves' liver, substitute with pigs' or lambs' liver. This is delicious served with polenta, or mashed potatoes, if you prefer.

Cooking time: 25 minutes (not including prep)

Serves 4

20 g/¾ oz/1 tbsp sultanas (golden raisins)
100 ml/3½ fl oz/7 tbsp white wine
4 tbsp extra-virgin olive oil
2 tbsp butter
2 large onions, finely sliced
sea salt and freshly ground black pepper
450 g/1 lb calves' liver, cut into finger slices
a handful of parsley, finely chopped

For the polenta:
800 ml/28 fl oz/3½ cups water
200 g/7 oz/1⅓ cups quick-cook polenta (fine cornmeal)
a knob (pat) of butter
sea salt, to taste

Soak the sultanas in the wine and set aside.

Heat the olive oil and butter in a frying pan (skillet) set over a low–medium heat. Add the onions and sweat for about 2 minutes. Add 2 tablespoons of water, season with some salt and pepper, cover with a lid, and cook over a gentle heat for 10 minutes, until the onions have softened but not browned. Remove the onions and set aside.

Increase the heat under the pan to medium–high, add the pieces of liver, season with some salt and pepper and cook to seal well. Cover with a lid, reduce the heat to low–medium, and cook for about 7 minutes.

Meanwhile, make the polenta. Heat the water in a saucepan and cook the polenta, (checking the instructions on your packet), adding a knob of butter and a little salt at the end.

Increase the heat under the frying pan with the liver, add the soaked sultanas and white wine and cook off for a minute. Add the parsley and onions, heat through for a minute or so, then serve with the polenta.

INVOLTINI DI MAIALE

PORK INVOLTINI

These quick, rolled pork *involtini,* packed full of herbs and garlic, remind me of the delicious flavours of a *porchetta.* Try to get the thinnest pork steaks you can, or ask your butcher to thinly cut and flatten them with a meat mallet, to save you time at home. They are delicious served with some boiled potatoes and a green salad.

Cooking time: 30 minutes (including prep)

Serves 2–4

4 thinly-cut pork escalopes or loin steaks
   (about 140 g/5 oz each)
sea salt and freshly ground black pepper
a handful of sage leaves, very finely chopped
needles of 1 rosemary sprig, very finely
   chopped
2 garlic cloves, very finely chopped
zest of ½ lemon
10 g/¼ oz/5 tbsp grated Parmesan
2 tbsp extra-virgin olive oil
60 ml/2 fl oz/4 tbsp white wine

Lay the pork escalopes/steaks out on a board, remove any excess fat and flatten as thinly as you can with a meat mallet. Season with salt and pepper, and scatter the meat with the chopped herbs and garlic, followed by the lemon zest and grated Parmesan. Carefully roll up the pork slices to make 4 *involtini* and secure with cocktail sticks (toothpicks).

In a large frying pan (skillet) set over a high heat, heat the olive oil, add the pork *involtini,* and cook to seal well on all sides. Add the white wine, cover with a lid, reduce the heat and cook for 15 minutes. Remove from the heat and serve the *involtini* with the pan juices.

SCALOPPINE DI VITELLO CON PORRI E ARANCIE SANGUINELLO

PAN-FRIED VEAL WITH LEEKS AND BLOOD ORANGES

Veal *scaloppine* are very popular in Italy for a quick and easy meal, traditionally pan-fried with butter, sage and lemon. As an alternative, I have used fresh thyme and delicious Sicilian blood oranges, which gives the meat a lovely, tangy kick! Unfortunately, blood-red oranges are only available during the months of January and February, so, if making out of season, just substitute with regular oranges. The addition of leeks here means you don't have to prepare a side vegetable. Serve with lots of good crusty bread to mop up the delicious sauce.

Cooking time: 20 minutes

Serves 4

5 small blood oranges (zest of 2 oranges, juice
    of 1 orange; break the remaining 4 oranges
    into segments)
2 tbsp plain (all-purpose) flour
sea salt and freshly ground black pepper
4 veal escalopes (about 100 g/3½ oz each)
120 g/4¼ oz/8 tbsp butter
2 leeks, trimmed and finely sliced
4 fresh thyme sprigs
100 ml/3½ fl oz/7 tbsp white wine

In a bowl, combine the orange zest with the flour, season with some salt and pepper, and set aside.

Lay the veal escalopes out flat on a board, flatten out further with a meat mallet, if necessary, and coat with the flour mixture, shaking off the excess. Set aside.

Melt 60 g/2¼ oz/4 tablespoons of the butter in a large frying pan (skillet) set over a medium heat. Add the leeks and sweat for 1 minute. Remove and set aside.

In the same pan, melt the remaining butter over a medium heat, add the thyme and leave to infuse for 1 minute. Increase the heat, add the veal and cook to seal well on both sides. Keep moving the meat around the pan to avoid burning. Pour in the wine and allow to evaporate by about half. Return the leeks to the pan, add the orange juice and half of the orange segments, and cook for 1 minute or so until the sauce begins to thicken slightly. Remove the meat, place on a serving dish and pour over the sauce. Serve immediately, garnished with the remaining fresh orange segments.

INVOLTINI DI BRESAOLA CON CAPRINO

BRESAOLA PARCELS FILLED WITH GOAT'S CHEESE AND CHIVES

Bresaola is a lovely cured beef that comes from the Valtellina area of northern Italy. Delicate in taste and extremely healthy, it is usually served as an antipasto with rocket (arugula), Parmesan, a drizzle of extra-virgin olive oil and lemon juice. Here, to enrich the cured beef, a delicious mixture of goat's cheese is added. This can be served as a quick antipasto or as a light main course.

Cooking time: 10 minutes

Serves 4

120 g/4¼ oz soft goat's cheese
1 tbsp extra-virgin olive oil,
    plus extra for drizzling
a handful of chives, finely chopped
sea salt and freshly ground black pepper
8 small slices of *bresaola* (about 50 g/1¾ oz
    in total)
juice of 1 lemon
8 whole chives, soaked
rocket (arugula) leaves, to serve

In a bowl, combine the cheese, olive oil and chives, seasoning with some salt and pepper, until creamy.

Place the slices of *bresaola* on a board or work surface and squeeze a little lemon juice over them. Place a small dollop of the creamy cheese mixture on each slice and wrap like a little parcel. Tie a soaked chive around each parcel to hold everything in place. Serve with rocket leaves, a drizzle of extra-virgin olive oil and another drizzle of lemon juice.

FILETTI DI POLLO IN PADELLA

PAN-FRIED MINI CHICKEN FILLETS

Mini chicken fillets, widely available in supermarkets, are very versatile and quick to cook. They can be added to stir-fries, made into quick stews or dipped in egg and coated with breadcrumbs for the best home-made chicken nuggets. This is a quick, lighter version of a classic Chicken *Cacciatora*. Serve with some good country-style bread or boiled baby potatoes. For extra speed, look out for ready-chopped fresh vegetables.

Cooking time: 25 minutes (including prep)

Serves 4

3 tbsp extra-virgin olive oil
1 onion, finely sliced
½ fresh red chilli, finely chopped
2 celery stalks, finely chopped
1 large carrot, finely chopped
2 rosemary sprigs
500 g/1 lb 2 oz mini chicken fillets
sea salt and freshly ground black pepper
80 ml/2½ fl oz/5 tbsp white wine
200 g/7 oz baby plum tomatoes
a handful of basil leaves

Heat the olive oil in a frying pan (skillet) set over a medium heat. Add the onion, chilli, celery, carrot and rosemary, and sweat for 2–3 minutes. Add the chicken fillets, season with some salt and pepper, and stir-fry until sealed on all sides. Add the white wine and allow the alcohol to evaporate. Add the tomatoes and basil, reduce the heat, cover with a lid, and cook for 12–15 minutes, until the chicken has cooked through.

POLPETTONE FARCITO

ADRIANA'S FILLED MEATLOAF

This dish reminds me of home, where we would often have meatballs. However, meatballs take a little time to make, patiently rolling each one individually. When my mother was in a hurry, she would make a meatloaf with minced (ground) meat instead. This is my sister Adriana's version, filled with delicious mortadella, mozzarella and hard-boiled eggs. Simple to prepare, it makes a nutritious meal, served with boiled baby potatoes and a green salad.

Cooking time: 40 minutes

Serves 4

3 eggs
250 g/9 oz good-quality minced beef steak
60 g/2¼ oz stale bread, soaked in a little milk
10 g/¼ oz/5 tbsp grated Parmesan
1 tbsp parsley, finely chopped
needles of 1 rosemary sprig, finely chopped
sea salt and freshly ground black pepper
2 slices of mortadella (about 25 g/1 oz in total)
70 g/2½ oz hard mozzarella, thinly sliced
egg wash, made with 1 egg yolk and
    1 tbsp milk
breadcrumbs, for coating

ready-made loaf tin (pan) liner

Preheat the oven to 220°C fan/240°C/475°F/gas mark 9, or your highest setting.

Boil 2 of the eggs until hard-boiled (about 7–8 minutes). When cooked, drain, remove the shells and slice lengthways in half.

In the meantime, combine the minced beef, bread, Parmesan, parsley, rosemary and 1 egg, seasoning with some salt and pepper. Place a piece of clingfilm (plastic wrap) on the work surface and spread the minced beef mixture on top, spreading it out into a flat rectangular shape. Lay over the mortadella slices, then the mozzarella slices, and top with the hard-boiled eggs. With the help of the clingfilm, roll up into a sausage shape, then carefully remove the clingfilm and discard it.

Brush egg wash all over the meatloaf and coat with the breadcrumbs. Place in a ready-made loaf tin (pan) liner (this helps the meatloaf to keep its shape) and place onto a baking (oven) tray. Roast in the hot oven for 25 minutes, reducing the oven temperature to 200°C fan/220°C/425°F/gas mark 7 after 10 minutes.

Remove from the oven and serve with boiled baby potatoes and a green salad.

BISTECCHE IN SALSA
STEAKS IN A HERB-INFUSED TOMATO SAUCE

When I was a child, this dish was often made as a quick supper during the late summer months, when tomatoes were ripe, ready and at their best. Nowadays, people cook this classic southern-Italian dish with canned tomatoes all year round. If you cook some pasta separately to serve, it makes a really quick two-course meal for all the family to enjoy.

Cooking time: 25–30 minutes

Serves 4

4 quick-cook, thin beef steaks
3 tbsp extra-virgin olive oil
1 large garlic clove, finely chopped
1 tsp capers
60 g/2¼ oz stoned (pitted) green olives
1 × 400-g/14-oz can of chopped tomatoes
a handful of basil leaves, plus a few extra to
    garnish (optional)
2 thyme sprigs
1 tsp dried oregano
sea salt and freshly ground black pepper
400 g/14 oz pasta of your choice

Heat the olive oil in a large frying pan (skillet) set over a medium heat. Add the steaks and cook to seal well on both sides, then remove and set aside.

In the same pan, add the garlic and sweat for about 30 seconds, stir in the capers and olives and continue to sweat for another 30 seconds. Add the tomatoes, basil, thyme and oregano, season with salt and pepper, and cook for a further 2 minutes. Return the steaks to the pan, cover with a lid and continue to cook over a medium heat for 20 minutes.

While the meat is cooking in the tomato sauce, bring a saucepan of salted water to the boil and cook some pasta. Serve the cooked pasta stirred though the tomato and olive sauce, with the meat as a main course. Garnish with a few extra chopped basil leaves, if wished.

VEGETABLES

Italy is blessed with a wonderful variety of vegetables, and each region has its own locally-grown varieties which, in season, are excellent for the traditional dishes of that particular area. The Mediterranean climate and the difference between the cooler north and warmer south makes it ideal for growing all sorts of different produce – the north has its root vegetables and the south its tomatoes, (bell) peppers, aubergines (eggplants) and more.

Italians don't just eat veggies as a side dish, although there is always seasonal veg or salad served at the table – we make wonderful main course dishes out of them too. Born from the *cucina povera*, in the days when poor people had to make do with the few ingredients they had available to them, wonderful dishes were created. Vegetables were often filled with leftovers and stale bread and made into substantial main courses – these dishes are still popular today and have become real delicacies.

Vegetables are quick to cook, are very versatile and can be made into delicious side dishes and main meals in no time. They provide lots of vital nutrients and vitamins and, quite frankly, I don't know how I could live without them.

Even though I prefer to eat seasonally – not only are veggies more economical that way, but they taste better too – we are lucky to find all sorts of produce available at almost any time of the year, which makes cooking dishes much easier. And when you're really under pressure time-wise, you can buy pre-prepared veg, such as trimmed green beans or chopped peppers, which can just go straight into the pan and save much preparation time.

FRITTATA CON PISELLI, PECORINO E MENTA

FRITTATA WITH PEAS, PECORINO AND FRESH MINT

Italians often have frittata for an evening meal (usually as a main course after a plate of pasta or soup). Frittata is nutritious, quick and easy to make, and can be enjoyed cold the next day as a *panino* – in between some bread. Serve with Oregano-Infused Mixed Tomato Salad (see p.28) for a healthy supper.

Cooking time: 15 minutes

Serves 4

3 tbsp extra-virgin olive oil
2 large *cipollotti* (extra-large spring onions/
    scallions), finely chopped
12 mint leaves
300 g/10½ oz frozen peas
1 tbsp water
8 eggs
2 tbsp milk
1 tbsp breadcrumbs
40 g/1½ oz/generous ½ cup grated Pecorino
sea salt and freshly ground black pepper,
    to taste

Heat the olive oil in a large, non-stick frying pan (skillet) set over a medium heat. Add the onions and a couple of mint leaves and sweat for 2 minutes. Stir in the peas and water and cook for 2–3 minutes, until the liquid has evaporated and the peas are tender.

Meanwhile, combine the eggs, milk, breadcrumbs, Pecorino, the remaining mint leaves, and some salt and pepper. Pour the eggy mixture over the peas and cook as you would an omelette, turning halfway through, until set firm and golden. If you find you can't turn the frittata over, place under a hot grill (broiler) for a few minutes, until golden and cooked.

VERDURE MISTE STUFATE

MIXED VEGGIE STEW

This quick, delicious vegetable stew can be served as an accompaniment to meat dishes or can be eaten as a main course with some steamed rice or bread. If you are in a hurry, most of these vegetables can be found ready-chopped in lots of supermarkets.

Cooking time: 25 minutes (not including veg prep)

Serves 4

3 tbsp extra-virgin olive oil
1 small red onion, finely sliced
1 small carrot, finely chopped
½ red (bell) pepper, finely chopped into
    thin strips
½ yellow (bell) pepper, finely chopped into
    thin strips
½ green (bell) pepper, finely chopped into
    thin strips
200 g/7 oz ripe tomatoes, roughly chopped
100 g/3½ oz fine green (French) beans,
    trimmed
200 g/7 oz courgettes (zucchini), finely sliced
200 g/7 oz aubergine (eggplant), finely
    chopped into small cubes
1 medium-sized potato, peeled and cut into
    small chunks
2 rosemary sprigs
2 thyme sprigs
1 tsp black peppercorns
200 ml/7 fl oz/scant 1 cup vegetable stock
    (bouillon)
½ handful of parsley, roughly chopped

Heat the olive oil in an extra-large saucepan set over a medium heat. Add the onion and sweat for 2 minutes. Stir in all the other vegetables, rosemary, thyme and peppercorns and cook for 1 minute or so, to allow the flavours to infuse. Pour in the stock, cover with a lid, and cook for 20 minutes.

Check the stew about 5 minutes before the end of the cooking time. If you find there is still too much liquid, increase the heat and cook uncovered, so that the liquid can reduce slightly. Remove from the heat, stir in the chopped parsley and serve.

ZUCCHINI IN POMODORO
COURGETTES IN TOMATO

Courgettes (zucchini) can be quite bland, so cooking them in a little tomato sauce gives them the kick they need to make a tasty side dish. It can be served with meat dishes or by itself with some crusty bread.

Cooking time: 25 minutes

Serves 4

2 tbsp extra-virgin olive oil
1 onion, finely chopped
50 g/1¾ oz/⅓ cup diced pancetta
500 g/1 lb 2 oz courgettes (zucchini), cut into
    small chunks
6 basil leaves
200 g/7 oz canned chopped tomatoes
sea salt and freshly ground black pepper

Heat the olive oil in a large saucepan set over a medium heat. Add the onion and pancetta and stir-fry for about 4 minutes, until the onion has softened and the pancetta has coloured a little. Stir in the courgettes and basil and stir-fry for 1 minute. Add the tomatoes, season with some salt and pepper, cover with a lid and cook over a low heat for about 10–15 minutes, stirring from time to time, until the courgettes are tender.

PIZZA VELOCE AL PANE CARASAU

QUICK PIZZA WITH SARDINIAN CRISPY BREAD

Pane Carasau, also known as *Carta di Musica*, is a crispy, unleavened flatbread, which was made for Sardinian shepherds to take with them to the mountains to eat during their working day. Its crispiness makes it a light alternative to bread, and its long shelf life makes it an ideal store-cupboard ingredient. You can find it in your local Italian deli.

This quick, pizza-type recipe makes a great snack when time is precious or for when impromptu guests appear. The addition of potatoes makes it quite filling, but you could use any of your favourite pizza toppings. When serving, I find a sharp pair of kitchen scissors the best tool to cut it with, as the bread is quite crispy.

Cooking time: 20–25 minutes (including prep)

Makes 2 large pizzas

600 g/1 lb 5 oz potatoes, peeled
  and thinly sliced
sea salt
1 red onion, finely sliced
a pinch of oregano
100 g/3½ oz cherry tomatoes, quartered
extra-virgin olive oil, for drizzling
2 large *pane carasau* (from your local
  Italian deli)
100 g/3½ oz mozzarella, roughly chopped

Preheat the oven to 180°C fan/200°C/400°F/gas mark 6.

Place the sliced potatoes in a saucepan of salted boiling water and cook for 5–6 minutes, until tender, but not falling apart. Drain well, taking care not to break them.

Meanwhile, prepare the other ingredients. Combine the sliced onion in a bowl with a little seasoning of salt and oregano. Mix the tomatoes in a bowl with a little salt and a drizzle of extra-virgin olive oil.

Place each *pane carasau* on a large flat baking tray (cookie sheet) and drizzle each with a little extra-virgin olive oil. Place the sliced potatoes on top, followed by some onions, mozzarella, and tomatoes, finishing off with another drizzle of olive oil. Place in the hot oven for 6–8 minutes, until the mozzarella has melted, and serve immediately.

PATATE AL PARMIGIANO E ROSMARINO

PARMESAN ROAST POTATOES WITH ROSEMARY

This is an alternative but wonderful way to serve roast potatoes. The Parmesan and polenta mixture adds a nice crunchiness, and the roasted rosemary is delicious to eat, as well as giving the dish a fantastic flavour. To cook this even more quickly, chop the potatoes into smaller chunks. It makes a lovely accompaniment to steaks and meat cutlets.

Cooking time: 30–35 minutes

Serves 4–6

1 kg/2 lb 4 oz potatoes, peeled and cut into
   small chunks
50 g/1¾ oz/¾ cup grated Parmesan
100 g/3½ oz/⅔ cup polenta flour (cornmeal or
   maize flour)
sea salt and freshly ground black pepper
2 tbsp extra-virgin olive oil,
   plus extra for drizzling
needles of 2 rosemary sprigs

Preheat the oven to 200°C fan/220°C/425°F/gas mark 7.

Place the potatoes in a large saucepan of water, bring to the boil and parboil for 5–6 minutes.

Meanwhile, combine the Parmesan and polenta flour with some salt and pepper in a bowl, and set aside.

Drain the potatoes well and let them steam-dry for a minute or so over a low heat to eliminate the excess moisture.

Add the olive oil to a roasting (oven) dish, add the potatoes and mix well to coat the potatoes in oil. Add the Parmesan mixture and mix again, until the potatoes are well coated. Scatter in the rosemary and drizzle with some more olive oil.

Place in the hot oven and roast for about 25 minutes, until cooked through and golden.

CAVOLFIORE AL FORNO
ROASTED CAULIFLOWER WITH LEMON, PAPRIKA AND BAY LEAVES

I love cauliflower and enjoy cooking it in many different ways. Roasting this root vegetable is now becoming popular in Italy, and exotic spices are often used as flavouring. This is my own version, using Italian ingredients and some paprika. For an added kick, you could substitute the paprika with dried chilli (hot red pepper) flakes. Quick and simple to prepare, it makes a lovely side to meat dishes, or, if you're like me, it's delicious to eat on its own!

Cooking time: 30 minutes (including prep)

Serves 4–6

500 g/1 lb 2 oz cauliflower florets
2 bay leaves, finely chopped
3 garlic cloves, left whole and squashed
2 tsp smoked paprika (pimentón)
sea salt
juice of 1 lemon
4 tbsp extra-virgin olive oil

Preheat the oven to 180°C fan/200°C/400°F/gas mark 6.

Combine all the ingredients in an ovenproof dish and roast in the hot oven for 25 minutes, until cooked through.

AGRODOLCE DI VERDURE AL ZAFFERANO

SAFFRON-INFUSED AGRODOLCE VEGETABLE STIR-FRY

The slightly sweet and sour flavour of the vinegar and sugar here gives a nice kick to the vegetables, and the saffron adds a hint of colour. This makes a lovely accompaniment to grilled meat, but is also delicious eaten on its own.

Cooking time: 25 minutes (including prep)

Serves 4

5 tbsp extra-virgin olive oil
2 garlic cloves, left whole and squashed
1 large red onion, finely sliced
120 g/4¼ oz celery heart, sliced
300 g/10½ oz rainbow chard, sliced
250 g/9 oz turnips, peeled and diced
170 g/6 oz long-stemmed broccoli, trimmed
3 tbsp white wine vinegar
2 tsp granulated sugar
a pinch of saffron strands

Heat 2 tablespoons of the olive oil in a small frying pan (skillet) set over a low heat. Add the garlic and onions and gently sweat for about 7 minutes.

At the same time, in a larger frying pan set over a medium–high heat, heat the rest of the olive oil, add the celery, rainbow chard, turnips and broccoli and stir-fry for about 10 minutes.

Combine the white wine vinegar, sugar and saffron, pour over the vegetables and allow to cook off. Stir in the onion (discard the garlic), and heat through for a final minute, before serving.

CAPPUCCIA POVERA AL FORNO

POOR MAN'S CABBAGE BAKE

This recipe is so typical of the days of *cucina povera*, when poor people made do with whatever ingredients were available to them, and bread was often used to make a meal go further. Simple, but nutritious, this can be served as a side dish to meat, but is just as delicious eaten as a main course.

Cooking time: 40 minutes (including prep)

Serves 2–4

1 hispi (spring or sweetheart) cabbage,
   roughly chopped into thick strips
sea salt
100 g/3½ oz country-style bread,
   such as sourdough
125 g/4½ oz mozzarella
3 tbsp extra-virgin olive oil,
   plus extra for drizzling
1 garlic clove, left whole
a few pinches of paprika

Preheat the oven to 180°C fan/200°C/400°F/gas mark 6.

Cook the cabbage in salted boiling water for about 7 minutes, then drain (keeping a ladle or so of the cooking water).

Meanwhile, chop the bread into cubes, and roughly slice the mozzarella, and set aside.

Heat the olive oil in a frying pan (skillet) set over a medium heat. Add the garlic and sweat for a minute or so. Add the drained cabbage to the pan, seasoning with a little salt and a pinch of paprika, and stir-fry for 4 minutes.

Place the cooked cabbage, bread cubes and mozzarella in an ovenproof dish, add a ladle of cooking water, a drizzle of olive oil and a sprinkle of paprika, and bake in the hot oven for 20 minutes.

Meanwhile heat the grill (broiler).

Remove the dish of baked cabbage from the oven and place under the hot grill for 4 minutes, until golden-brown. Serve immediately.

TORTINO DI BIETOLE CON UOVA
BREAKFAST, LUNCH AND DINNER!

A delicious bake of chard, eggs and cheese, the English title of this recipe sums up the fact that you can enjoy this dish at any time of day! Very quick and simple to prepare, it makes a nutritious breakfast as well as a light supper. Be careful not to add salt to the creamy mixture, because the olive paste tends to be quite salty already. If you prefer, you could omit the olive paste and serve the toasted bread with a little salt and a drizzle of extra-virgin olive oil instead.

Cooking time: 20 minutes (including prep)

Serves 4

400 g/14 oz rainbow chard, washed
   and trimmed
sea salt, for the cooking water
butter, for greasing
small jar of black olive paste
4 eggs, carefully separated (try to keep the
   yolks whole)
100 ml/3½ fl oz/7 tbsp double (heavy) cream
freshly ground black pepper, to taste
40 g/1½ oz/generous ½ cup grated Parmesan
slices of sourdough bread, to serve

4 × 15-cm/6-in round terracotta dishes

Preheat the oven to 160°C fan/180°C/350°F/gas mark 4.

Add the chard to a saucepan of salted boiling water and cook for 5 minutes.

Meanwhile, grease 4 × 15-cm/6-in round terracotta dishes with butter and spread a little of the black olive paste, to taste, in the bottom of each.

Whisk together the egg whites, double cream, black pepper and grated Parmesan, until well combined and creamy.

Drain the chard and divide between the terracotta dishes, overlapping the leaves if necessary to fit into the dishes. Pour over the creamy mixture and bake in the hot oven for 7 minutes. After this time, remove from the oven and carefully add an egg yolk on top of each dish. Return to the oven for 2–3 minutes, until the egg is cooked but still soft.

Lightly toast the bread slices, spread with a little of the olive paste and serve with the egg and chard bakes.

LATTUGA RIPIENA

FILLED GEM LETTUCE

In Southern Italy, where *escarole* – a type of lettuce – is widely grown, it is quite common to serve it like this. The idea originated in the days of *cucina povera* (peasant cooking), when local vegetables would be filled with whatever ingredients were available, to make the meal go further. These crunchy Gem lettuces can be served as a starter, side or main.

Cooking time: 20 minutes

Serves 2–4

1 tbsp extra-virgin olive oil,
   plus extra for drizzling
1 garlic clove, left whole
½ fresh red chilli, finely chopped
100 g/3½ oz/1¾ cups shop-bought
   breadcrumbs
30 g/1 oz pine nuts
salt and freshly ground black pepper
60 g/2¼ oz/½ cup mixed green and black
   stoned (pitted) olives, sliced in half or in
   quarters, depending on size
2 Gem lettuces, as large as you can find

Preheat the oven to 180°C fan/200°C/400°F/gas mark 6.

Heat a frying pan (skillet) over a low-medium heat, add the olive oil, then add the garlic and chilli and cook for 1 minute, being careful not to let them burn. Add the breadcrumbs and pine nuts and cook for 3 minutes, until lightly toasted. Remove from the heat, discard the garlic clove, then stir in the olives. Season with a little salt and pepper.

Slightly open each Gem lettuce and fill with the breadcrumb mixture, tucking it down in the centre and in between the leaves. Place each lettuce on a sheet of baking (parchment) paper, drizzle all over with some olive oil, then wrap the lettuce up tightly in the paper – like a huge boiled sweet (hard candy)! Place on a baking tray (cookie sheet) and bake in the hot oven for 8 minutes.

Remove from the oven and carefully open the parcels. Slice the lettuces in half lengthways and serve.

FAGIOLINI IN UOVO AL SUCCO DI LIMONE

EGGY GREEN BEANS WITH LEMON

I remember seeing this dish made at a farmhouse in Puglia – the green beans were freshly picked from their garden and the eggs were fresh from their chickens. I remember thinking it was such a simple recipe, but the flavours were out of this world. I have tried to recreate it for this book. Although it is typically served as a side dish to meat, I could quite happily eat a bowlful with some country bread.

Cooking time: 20 minutes

Serves 4

500 g/1 lb 2 oz green (French) beans, trimmed
1 generous tbsp butter
1 tbsp extra-virgin olive oil
sea salt and freshly ground black pepper
1 egg, lightly beaten
juice of ½ lemon

Cook the beans in boiling water for 10–15 minutes, until tender, then drain.

In a large frying pan (skillet), heat the butter and olive oil over a high heat, add the drained beans, season with salt and pepper and stir-fry for 1 minute. Reduce the heat to medium, then add the beaten egg and lemon juice, stirring well. Remove from the heat and serve immediately.

SIMPLE SAUCES

Delicious Italian food can be prepared in an instant by adding tomato sauce or pesto to quickly prepared meat, fish and vegetable dishes, pasta, soups and salads. In this section are two of my favourite sauce recipes to make ahead and store, or, if you need to make a sauce in a hurry, to adorn whatever you are preparing.

SALSA AL POMODORO
BASIC TOMATO SAUCE

There are so many good-quality tomato sauces on the market now, especially the fresh ones sold in Italian delis, but I always like to make my own. This is my version of a plain, simple tomato sauce, which can be used to dress pasta or add to many other dishes. When you have time, it's always worth making a batch or two to freeze and use later. It will keep fresh in the fridge for up to 3 days.

Cooking time: 25 minutes, including prep time

Makes approx. 680 g/1 lb 8 oz/3 cups

2 tbsp extra-virgin olive oil
½ onion, finely chopped
2 × 400-g/14-oz tins of chopped plum
    tomatoes
sea salt, to taste
handful of basil, roughly torn

Heat the olive oil in a saucepan set over a medium heat, add the chopped onion and sweat for a couple of minutes. Add the chopped tomatoes and some water (about half a tomato can), some salt to taste, and the basil. Cover the pan with a lid and simmer on a low–medium heat for about 20 minutes. Check for seasoning and use accordingly.

PESTO
PESTO SAUCE

Pesto is always handy to keep in the fridge so you can whip up a quick meal in no time.
Add it to cooked pasta or gnocchi, liven up vegetable soups, add to omelettes or simply use
it in sandwiches. It will keep in the fridge for about a week or it can be frozen. If you store pesto
in the fridge, make sure you add some extra-virgin olive oil over the top and cover with clingfilm
(plastic wrap) to preserve it. I usually make pesto the old-fashioned way with a pestle and
mortar, which doesn't take that long and means the pesto retains a slight crunchiness, but
you can also whiz it in a food processor, which takes no time at all.

Cooking time: 15 minutes by hand/5 minutes in a food processor

Makes 4 servings, to dress pasta or gnocchi

2 tbsp pine nuts
1 garlic clove
½ tsp coarse sea salt
80 g/2¾ oz fresh basil leaves
   (discard the stalks)
200 ml/7 fl oz/scant 1 cup good-quality
   extra-virgin olive oil
2 tbsp freshly grated Parmesan

Put the pine nuts, garlic and sea salt into a mortar and grind with a pestle. Add a few basil leaves
and some olive oil, grinding and stirring with the pestle. Continue this procedure until you
have used up all the basil leaves and about half of the olive oil and have obtained a smooth, silky
consistency. Add the remaining olive oil and the Parmesan and combine well.

Alternatively, place all the ingredients in a food processor and blend.

DESSERTS

When planning meals, people often overlook desserts, thinking they take too long or are just too hard to tackle, instead opting for a shop-bought pudding or cake. Desserts don't have to take a long time to prepare to be impressive or delicious – sometimes the quickest and simplest are the best.

I remember as a child, my favourite sweet treat was fresh ricotta simply combined with a little sugar and cinnamon or perhaps some chocolate chips or dried fruit. Ricotta is used in a lot of Italian desserts, as a filling for tarts and pies, or in classic pastries such as Sicilian *cannoli* and *cassata*. More recently, mascarpone – the rich, creamy cheese used to make tiramisu – has taken over in popularity and this, too, is now added to many desserts.

Fruit has always been a popular dessert in Italy and most families will offer a bowl of seasonal fruit after a meal for everyone to help themselves to. Fruit is good for you, is packed with vitamins, provides a natural source of sugar, and is often included in many Italian tarts and cakes. The classic *macedonia di frutta* (fruit salad), drizzled with a little freshly squeezed lemon or orange juice, is always a welcome dessert in Italy – it takes little time to prepare and provides a healthy, light and refreshing end to a meal.

I hope you will enjoy recreating my quick and simple pudding ideas, all of which can be made just before serving. Most can also be prepared in advance, if you prefer.

AMARETTI RIPIENI

FILLED SOFT AMARETTI

Soft amaretti, or *amaretti morbidi* in Italian, are like little cakes and are not to be confused with the hard, crispy variety of amaretti. Made with ground almonds, they are gluten-free (although always check the packet) and are obtainable in Italian delis or in larger supermarkets. They are delicious eaten on their own; filled with a rich, creamy centre, they also make a lovely, quick dessert. If you can't find raw pistachios, substitute with walnuts, chocolate chips, candied fruit, or a combination, if desired.

Cooking time: 20 minutes (including prep)

Makes 12–24 (depending on size!)

20 g/¾ oz/2½ tbsp raw pistachios
75 g/2½ oz/⅓ cup ricotta
75 g/2½ oz/⅓ cup mascarpone
15 g/½ oz/1 generous tbsp caster (superfine)
    sugar
3 tsp Marsala wine, plus extra for brushing
20–24 soft amaretti biscuits (cookies)
a little icing (confectioners') sugar, for dusting

Toast the pistachios in a dry frying pan (skillet) set over a medium–high heat for a couple of minutes, until lightly toasted. Remove and set aside.

Meanwhile, whisk together the ricotta, mascarpone, sugar and Marsala wine in a bowl, until light and fluffy. Finely chop the pistachios and stir in. Cover with clingfilm (plastic wrap) and place in the fridge.

Using a really good, sharp knife, slice the amaretti horizontally in half, so you end up with a bottom and top of each little cake, keeping any crumbs. Brush each slice with a little Marsala. Take the creamy mixture out of the fridge and stir in the amaretti crumbs. Place a dollop of the cream on the bottom slice of the amaretti and sandwich together with the top half. Arrange on a plate and dust with icing sugar, to serve.

BUDINO AL CIOCCOLATO E LAMPONI

CHOCOLATE AND RASPBERRY POTS

These quick, soufflé-type chocolate puddings are so easy to make, they are almost child's play. But *shhh*, don't tell your guests – they'll think you've been slaving in the kitchen for hours when they taste them! You can prepare them in advance and pop them in the microwave for about 20–30 seconds each, just before serving. Make sure you use good-quality, organic dark (bittersweet) chocolate and fresh raspberries. Simply eat with a spoon, straight out of the ramekin or cup!

Cooking time: 25 minutes

Serves 4

65 g/2¼ oz/4 tbsp butter,
   plus extra for greasing
125 g/4½ oz/4½ squares dark chocolate,
   broken into pieces
3 eggs, separated (keep 2 egg yolks,
   1 can be saved for later or discarded)
25 g/1 oz/2 tbsp caster (superfine) sugar
a pinch of table salt
100 g/3½ oz raspberries

Preheat the oven to 160°C fan/180°C/350°F/gas mark 4. Lightly grease 4 ramekins or cappuccino cups, place them on a flat baking tray and set aside.

Melt the chocolate pieces and butter in a heatproof bowl set over a pan of gently simmering water. Make sure the base of the bowl doesn't touch the water.

Meanwhile, in another bowl, whisk 2 egg yolks with 15 g/½ oz/1 generous tablespoon of sugar, until light and creamy.

In another very clean bowl, whisk the 3 egg whites with the remaining sugar and a pinch of salt, until stiff.

Combine the melted chocolate mixture with the egg yolk mixture. Now, fold in the stiffened egg whites, until well incorporated. Pour into the prepared ramekins/cups up to about halfway, gently place 3–4 raspberries in each, pushing them in a little, then pour the remaining chocolate mixture over to cover. Bake in the hot oven for 6 minutes. Remove and serve.

SORBETTO DI FRUTTI DI BOSCO VELOCE
QUICK MIXED BERRY SORBET

Quick and easy to make, this sorbet is made with frozen mixed berries, which are widely obtainable in supermarkets. Alternatively, you can freeze the berries that you pick or grow yourself during the summer – they are always handy to have in the freezer, so you can whip up a healthy dessert at any time. My daughter Olivia loves this idea and makes sorbets of all kinds with different types of frozen fruit. I have given you a few serving suggestions, but you can adapt to whatever you prefer or simply enjoy the sorbet by itself.

Cooking time: 5 minutes

Serves 4–6

500 g/1 lb 2 oz frozen mixed berries
juice of 1 orange
100 g/3½ oz/generous ½ cup caster
　(superfine) sugar

Serving suggestions:
crushed amaretti biscuits (cookies)
Pavesini biscuits (Italian sponge cookies)
fresh fruit, e.g. sliced kiwi or mango chunks
crème fraîche or extra-thick double
　(heavy) cream

Place all the ingredients into a food processor and blend until smooth. Serve immediately, with the above serving suggestions or your own ideas.

CREMA DI MASCARPONE CON PERE E NOCI

MASCARPONE MOUSSE WITH PEAR AND WALNUTS

This is a very quick, simple and delicious dessert! The cream is quite indulgent and combines really well with my favourite fruit and nuts: soft, sweet pears and crunchy walnuts. A perfect dinner party dessert, this looks lovely served in glass bowls or glasses.

Cooking time: 10 minutes

Serves 4–6

5 ripe Conference pears, peeled and cored
40 g/1½ oz/⅓ cup walnut halves
250 g/9 oz/1 generous cup mascarpone
250 g/9 oz/1 generous cup soft cream cheese
100 ml/3½ fl oz/7 tbsp double (heavy) cream
25 g/1 oz/2 tbsp caster (superfine) sugar
runny honey, for drizzling

Chop 4 of the pears into small chunks and divide between 4–6 bowls or glasses. Slice the remaining pears into 4–6 pieces and set aside.

Roughly break up the walnuts, keeping 4–6 intact, for decoration. Place the broken walnut pieces in the bowls or glasses with the pears.

In a bowl, combine the mascarpone, cream cheese, double cream and sugar, and mix with a spoon until smooth. Spoon this creamy mixture over the chopped pears and walnuts in the bowls or glasses. Drizzle with a little runny honey and decorate with the remaining pieces of pear and walnuts. Serve immediately, or store in the fridge until required.

MERINGA CON CREMA DI LIMONE E FRUTTI DI BOSCO

MERINGUE NESTS WITH LEMON CUSTARD AND BERRIES

Ready-made meringue nests are widely available and, as they usually have a long sell-by-date, are great to keep in your store-cupboard to use for a speedy dessert. Meringue goes so well with this quick-to-prepare, lemon-infused custard. If you are in a hurry, you could omit the cooling time and just spoon the hot custard onto the nests. They are delicious and look really lovely.

Cooking time: 35–40 minutes (including cooling time)

Makes 6 nests

250 ml/9 fl oz/1 generous cup whole (full-fat) milk
5-cm/2-in piece of lemon peel
1 tbsp limoncello liqueur
3 egg yolks
50 g/1¾ oz/generous ¼ cup caster (superfine) sugar
30 g/1 oz/scant ¼ cup plain (all-purpose) flour, sifted
selection of fresh berries: strawberries, raspberries, blueberries, blackberries
6 ready-made meringue nests

Heat the milk, lemon peel and limoncello in a small saucepan set over a gentle heat – be careful not to boil.

Meanwhile, in a large bowl, whisk together the eggs yolks and caster sugar, until light and fluffy. Whisk in the sifted flour.

When the milk is hot, gradually pour into the egg mixture, whisking all the time. Return the mixture to the pan over a low–medium heat and cook, stirring well with a wooden spoon, until the custard thickens. Pour into a cold dish, remove the piece of lemon peel and leave to cool for about 15 minutes.

Slice the strawberries, if using, and arrange the meringue nests on a large serving plate or board. Once cool, place the custard cream into a piping bag and pipe onto the meringue nests – or you can just spoon it on. Top with the mixed berries and serve.

PESCHE AL PASSITO CON MASCARPONE
PASSITO-INFUSED PEACHES WITH MASCARPONE

For this dish, use the just-ripe, delicious, sweet peaches of early summer, when they are at their best. Delicious served warm, you can also prepare all the ingredients in advance and just heat the peaches through in the liquor before serving. The warm peaches go really well with the mascarpone cream, or you could serve with good-quality vanilla ice cream, if desired. *Passito di Pantelleria* is an exquisite dessert wine from the Sicilian island of Pantelleria. If you can't find it, substitute with Vin Santo, Marsala, or another sweet dessert wine.

Cooking time: 20–25 minutes (including prep)

Serves 4–6

6 tbsp *Passito di Pantelleria* or
   sweet dessert wine
2 tbsp freshly squeezed orange juice
40 g/1½ oz/scant ¼ cup light brown
   (muscovado) sugar
4 peaches
150 g/5½ oz mascarpone
20 g/¾ oz/scant ¼ cup icing (confectioners')
   sugar, sifted

Combine 5 tablespoons of the *Passito* with the orange juice and brown sugar, and set aside.

Place the peaches in boiling water for about 30 seconds. Remove with a slotted spoon and plunge straight into ice-cold water to cool them. Once cooled, use a paring knife to peel away the skin, then cut the peaches into segments, about 8 per peach. Place the peach segments into the *Passito* liquor and leave to macerate for 10 minutes.

Meanwhile, combine the mascarpone, icing sugar and remaining *Passito*, and set aside.

Place the macerated peaches and their liquor into a small saucepan, bring to the boil and simmer over a medium heat for 5 minutes. Carefully remove the peaches and divide between 4–6 dessert bowls or glasses. Return the liquor to the heat and cook over a high heat for a couple of minutes, until it reduces and thickens.

Top the peaches with dollops of the mascarpone mixture, drizzle over the reduced liquor and serve immediately.

GIRANDOLE ALLA CANNELLA

CINNAMON PUFFS

These are really easy and quick-to-make biscuits (cookies), which can be made at any time, then stored in an airtight container. They are delicious served at teatime. Try to get ready-rolled puff pastry, which will save you time rolling out. The ground cinnamon can be substituted with ground mixed spice.

Cooking time: 30 minutes

Makes about 15

325 g/11½ oz ready-rolled sheet of
   puff pastry
130 g/4¾ oz/⅔ cup soft light brown
   (light muscovado) sugar
3 tsp ground cinnamon
1 egg white, lightly beaten

Preheat the oven to 170°C fan/190°C/375°F/gas mark 5. Line a large, flat baking tray (cookie sheet) with parchment paper.

Combine the sugar and cinnamon in a bowl.

Unroll the puff pastry sheet and sprinkle about three-quarters of the sugar mixture all over. Roll the pastry up along the longest side, brush all over with the beaten egg white and sprinkle with the remaining sugar mixture. Cut the roll into approx. 2-cm/¾-in wide rounds, place them on the prepared baking tray and bake in the hot oven for 20 minutes, until golden.

MACEDONIA DI AGRUMI CON YOGURT SPEZIATO

CITRUS FRUIT SALAD WITH A CINNAMON YOGURT

This makes a lovely, healthy dessert, which is full of vitamin C! You can either serve the fruit in a large bowl with the yogurt on the side, for people to help themselves, or you can divide between individual bowls and dollop the yogurt on top. Add more cinnamon if you prefer.

Cooking time: 15 minutes (including prep time)

Serves 4–6

1 yellow grapefruit
1 pink grapefruit
2 oranges
juice and zest of 1 lime
a grating of fresh ginger
1 tbsp runny honey
200 g/7 oz/scant 1 cup plain yogurt
a pinch of ground cinnamon
mint leaves, to garnish

Peel the citrus fruit, removing as much of the white pith as possible, then split into segments and place in a bowl. Combine the lime juice, grated ginger and honey and pour over the fruit. Set aside.

Combine the yogurt and cinnamon. Divide the fruit between 4–6 bowls, top with the yogurt and garnish with lime zest and mint leaves, to serve.

TORTA AL TIRAMISU

TIRAMISU CAKE

This is a twist on the popular Italian dessert. The sponge is a classic *pan di Spagna,* often the basis of most Italian celebration cakes, which is brushed with espresso coffee and filled with a creamy mascarpone filling. It can be served as an after-dinner dessert or for teatime. If you are not serving it immediately, store it in the fridge until required.

Cooking time: 35–40 minutes

Serves 6–8

For the *pan di Spagna* sponge:
butter, for greasing the tins
3 eggs
90 g/3¼ oz/scant ½ cup caster (superfine)
 sugar
90 g/3¼ oz/scant ¾ cup plain (all-purpose)
 flour, sifted
a pinch of table salt
1 tsp vanilla extract

For the coffee:
150 ml/5 fl oz/scant ⅔ cup espresso coffee
1 tbsp caster (superfine) sugar
1 tbsp Marsala wine, Passito (Italian straw
 wine), or other liqueur

For the cream:
250 g/9 oz mascarpone
40 g/1½ oz/scant ¼ cup caster (superfine)
 sugar
2 egg yolks
125 ml/4 fl oz/½ cup double (heavy) cream
2 tbsp Marsala wine, or other liqueur

20 g/¾ oz dark (bittersweet) chocolate, grated,
 to decorate

Preheat the oven to 160°C fan/180°C/350°F/gas mark 4. Grease and line 2 × 19-cm/7½-in round cake tins (pans) with parchment paper or, for extra speed, use ready-made cake tin liners.

Prepare a pot of espresso coffee, take off the heat and set aside.

For the sponge, whisk the eggs and sugar together in a large bowl for about 5 minutes, until light and fluffy and the sugar has dissolved (to help speed up the process, add a drop of hot water). Fold in the flour, salt and vanilla extract. Pour into the prepared tins and bake in the hot oven for 17–20 minutes. Insert a skewer into the sponge to test it; if it comes out clean, the cake is done. Set aside to cool a little in the tins.

Meanwhile, combine the cooled espresso coffee, sugar and Marsala and set aside.

For the cream, whisk together the mascarpone, sugar, egg yolks and double cream in a bowl, until light and fluffy. Fold in the Marsala wine just before assembling the cake to avoid splitting the mixture.

Remove the sponges from the tins while still warm, but cool enough to handle. Remove the parchment paper/tin liners and, using a pastry brush, brush the coffee mixture over both sides of the sponges. Leave to soak in for about 5 minutes. Spread one of the sponges with about half of the cream mixture and sprinkle with some of the grated chocolate, then sandwich with the top layer of sponge. Spread the remaining cream over the top and sprinkle with the last of the chocolate.

TIRAMISU ALLE FRAGOLE DI ADRIANA

ADRIANA'S STRAWBERRY TIRAMISU

Light and summery, this is my sister's tiramisu recipe that she often makes for family occasions. It's perfect for kids, as it contains no coffee (and the alcohol is optional!) but is packed with lots of healthy fruit. You can serve it immediately or make it in advance and store in the fridge, if you prefer.

Cooking time: 25–30 minutes (including prep)

Serves 6

700 g/1 lb 9 oz strawberries, hulled
juice and zest of 1 lemon
1 tbsp limoncello liqueur (optional)
4 tbsp, plus 80 g/2¾ oz/scant ½ cup caster
   (superfine) sugar
4 egg yolks
200 g/7 oz/1 cup mascarpone
250 ml/9 fl oz/1 generous cup thickened
   double (heavy) cream
300 g/10½ oz savoiardi sponge fingers
   (ladyfinger biscuits)
100 g/3½ oz mixed berries
fresh mint (optional)

Roughly chop 500 g/1 lb 2 oz of the strawberries and combine with the lemon juice, limoncello (if using) and the 4 tablespoons of sugar, cover with clingfilm (plastic wrap), and place in the fridge while you prepare the creamy filling.

Whisk the egg yolks and 80 g/2¾ oz/scant ½ cup of sugar, until light and creamy. Add the mascarpone and continue to whisk until well amalgamated and creamy. Stir in the double cream and mix well with a spoon. Store in the fridge while you prepare the strawberry sauce.

Take the macerated strawberries out of the fridge and blend until smooth.

Line a deep serving dish or trifle bowl with a little of the creamy mixture. Dip the savoiardi into the strawberry sauce and arrange over the top of the creamy mixture. Spread more of the creamy mixture over the sponge fingers and continue making layers like this, until you have finished all the ingredients, ending with a cream layer. Decorate the top with the remaining whole strawberries, the mixed berries and a few sprigs of fresh mint if you have it. You can serve immediately, if wished, or pop it back in the fridge until you are ready.

INDEX

MY THANKS TO

Liz Przybylski for writing the recipes and chapter introductions; Adriana Contaldo for testing the recipes and cooking at the shoots; Kim Lightbody for beautiful photos; Becci Woods for lovely food styling; Alexander Breeze for selecting lovely props; Emily Preece-Morrison for editing; Stephanie Milner for all your help bringing everyone together; Laura Russell for the gorgeous design; Laura Brodie for supreme production; Komal Patel for getting the word out; Polly Powell for publishing this book and Luigi Bonomi for making it happen.